"What in tarnation is it?" the people asked.

They gathered around

and I displayed it in the palm of my hand.

"Ten holes. Twenty notes.  Blow and draw," I said.

"Teensy little thing," they laughed.

But once I started playing it for them,

they wouldn't let me stop.

# Harmonica Americana

## History, Instruction and Music for 30 Great American Tunes

by

## Jon Gindick

with illustrations by

## Art Ellis

typesetting & creative design by
**Diane Mountford**

**Cross Harp Press**
Visalia • Los Angeles

## Other books, cassettes, and videos by Jon Gindick

- Country and Blues Harmonica for the Musically Hopeless

- The Natural Blues and Country Western Harmonica

- Rock n' Blues Harmonica,
  Stories, Lessons, and Record Index

- Great American Harmonica Music

- First Note Harmonica for Children

- The Robert Johnson Songbook

- Gospel Plow Harmonica

- Country and Blues Harmonica for the Absolute Beginner
  (instructional video with B.B. King)

- Play the Harmonica Overnight (instructional video)

- Video Songbook
  (instructional video teaching many of the songs
  in this book)

**Harmonica Americana
is dedicated
to the artist in each of us.**

**Long may it live!**

## With special thanks to . . .

Art Ellis, my most excellent illustrator-editor-art director-book designer and fellow musician without whose patience, dedication, and mind-blowing talent this book would be far less than it is; Diane Mountford, typesetter-musician-actor who brought a special flair to every page; Tia Gindick-Lewis, publicist unparalleled; Jane Applegate and Peter Imber, for their good taste in stories; Dr. Craig Naylor, who came up with the title; Jack, Bill and Horst at Hohner for years of support and interest in my projects; Joe Vitale and Dale Scherfling, harp-buddies and fellow writers; Ric Guiterez, that "point of light," who provided moral support when changes were afoot; Debbie Andrus, whose help with the cover was invaluable; Kim Ellis, air brusher and color selector supreme; Mel Ellis of the New Britain Museum of American Art for letting a stranger touch greatness; and Michael Rey, Miguel Rivera, Walter Atkinson, Charles Bernstein, Alex Titchner, Sharon Mountford, Frank, G.A., Ritchie Lewis, Nicki, Molly Lee Dunn, Daniel Atyum and the Golden Age crowd who waited, waited and waited until this project was finally completed.

## About the Cover . . .

Thomas Hart Benton traveled the United States and depicted its enormous energy in his fantastic paintings and murals. A student of form, whose theories fill textbooks, his style, with its bold flowing lines, is distinctly musical. Although he was penniless almost until the age of forty, Benton lived well into his eighties and was widely recognized as one of our greatest American artists by the time he died.

In addition to painting, one of Benton's great loves was playing the harmonica. He released an album called "Saturday Night at Tom Benton's" in 1941, and devised his own method of harmonica notation which was commonly used for many years. The harmonica figures prominently in his series of paintings on American music and arts. The model for the harmonica player on the cover of **Harmonica Americana** was Jackson Pollack, an equally famous American painter, and Tom Benton's protegée.

# Who Can Learn to Play?  You Can!

As a teacher of the harmonica, I frequently receive letters from people asking, "I'm seventy-three (or sixty-three or eighty-three or forty-three) years old.  Is it too late for me to learn to play? "

I always wish I could introduce the writers of these letters to folks like Augusta, the seventy-seven year old woman with no prior musical experience who learned to play the blues, and went on to teach a class at a senior citizen center. Or to Hank, who, at age sixty-three started playing, and developed the same train imitation act he saw his grandfather use fifty years earlier. Or to the countless others I've known who overcame their doubts and satisfied the lifelong dream of being able to whip out a harmonica and make some music.

Obviously, the answer is "Of course you can learn to play."  Mostly, it depends on your attitude. If you're patient, if you're willing to have fun as you learn, and if you play everyday, your success as a harmonica student is something you can count on.  The only students who don't learn to play are those who quit. Those who stay with it **always** improve.

One way **Harmonica Americana** is different than my other books is that it teaches *songs* rather than blues. I've found that while many people grew up with blues and rock, others of us were raised on songs and would do anything to be able to play a few of the great ones on the mouth organ. Naturally that takes practice.

And what about practice? The answer is *yes!* During your initial harp-learning period,  Doc Gindick recommends fifteen to twenty minutes of harp-doodling a day—half in focused concentration, the other half in fooling around . The music gets into your head this way; and no matter what anyone says, most of learning to play any musical instrument, including the harmonica, is sub-conscious.

Another word of advice—*be your own biggest fan!* When practicing, tell yourself your music is sounding good. Use the exercises to turn problems into opportunities to learn to play better. And let yourself pretend that you're better than you already are. (More on this later.) Believe me, encouraging yourself with helpful self-talk and a vivid imagination is the best way to learn.

So get yourself a harp, pucker up, and don't let anyone tell you you're too young or too old to play harmonica.

Because you can do it.

Jon "Doc" Gindick, your teacher
Topanga, 1994

# TABLE OF CONTENTS

# AMERICANA SONGBOOK

# About the Songs . . .

*"Swing low, sweet chariot, coming for to carry me home . . ."*
*"Beautiful dreamer, come unto me . . ."*
*"Well, I had an old hen, and she had a wooden leg . . ."*

These are a few famous lines from the songs of **Harmonica Americana** and I'm proud to present them to you. From "Shenandoah" to "Yankee Doodle" to "Red River Valley" to "Turkey in the Straw," these informal, frequently improvised tunes are the seeds of American popular music. Their melodic format, musical structure and lyrical content pervade contemporary folk, blues, jazz, pop, soul, rock n' roll, country western and gospel. They are so common as to be considered cliches, yet if you don't know them "you don't know nuthin'."

Who wrote these songs? Who was it that sat down at a desk or piano (or with a harmonica), pulled out a fountain pen, scribbled those first tentative lyrics, or played a half-formed melody—a melody that would be sung by millions of men, women and children throughout the world for the next hundred years and beyond?

Songwriters like Stephen Foster, Dan Emmet, Sarah Sheppard, Francis Scott Key, George Bennard, Julia Ward Howe, John Phillip Sousa and Hughie Cannon are for most of us just names. And their music? Well, for me, songs like "Oh! Susannah" or "Dixie" or "Turkey in the Straw" are as natural as the American landscape. They are so well-known there's a tendency to take them for granted. An unfortunate tendency, because the goal of these songwriters was to give us songs we could live by, and they did exactly that.

Think about this for a moment. Can you imagine an America without "On Top of Old Smokey?" An America in which "Red River Valley," "Amazing Grace," "Dixie" or "Frankie and Johnny" were never hummed or sung or played? What would be missing? What would that silence be? The songs of **Harmonica Americana** are a living expression of the history of America. Some were written by those songwriters whose names we remember. Others are traditional, which means *natural,* written not by a specific writer, but shaped instead by the travels and travails of the times, cooked in the melting pots of English, French, African, Irish and American cultures and served up on the strings, reeds, keyboards and voices of our nation's musicians.

And why should we learn to play these songs? Because they are our tradition, a tradition that makes life rich. They bridge the generations, cultures, and the differences that seem so omnipresent in today's difficult world. Being able to lighten the load for others with a tune, to encourage them to sing along, or even to teach them to play the song themselves—all this brings people together, and touches our collective heart.

Moreover, learning to play the songs of **Harmonica Americana** is also an excellent way for **you** to learn harmonica. Many of these classics, sung since our childhoods, have worn a permanent groove into the mind of almost everyone. And if you can think it, you can play it. The idea is to pick up the harmonica, to remember that groove, and to fill it with your own musical impulse. Because you already know these songs, there's no formal music-reading, and little theory. All you have to do is *feel* the song, *believe* the song, add a little technique and *do it*.

Is it truly that easy? Well, if you're new to the game of making music, you may need to furrow out that musical groove a little bit. Throw out some of the rocks and debris of shyness and self-consciousness that are clogging the melodic flow in your mind. How? Try singing the songs. Hum if you don't feel like singing. If that doesn't work, think about someone else singing.

Always remember that the human voice is the basis of all music, especially the bending, wailing tones of the harp. Share this book with friends and family and get them to sing along with you. (Car rides are perfect for this.) Several people singing together almost always sounds better than one person. Lose those inhibitions— they may keep you out of trouble, but they won't help you make music.

Now at some point in your future harmonica playing career you may want to go further. You may want to improvise on these songs, learn more advanced harmonica styles, or even pick up another instrument such as guitar, banjo, dulcimer, fiddle or piano. That would be a wonderful development. But for now, limber your lips, pick up your harp and let's play the great old songs of **Harmonica Americana.**

# Chapter One

# Harmonica Americana

A brief, informal history of that
little piece of musical genius
commonly called "the harmonica," "the mouth organ"
and most affectionately "the harp."

*"I remember one time playing
'On Top of Ol' Smokey' as I was ridin'
some fifteen miles to town.  This cowboy came riding
up beside me and asked if he could ride along.
He saw me looking at him and said
he'd been planning to rob me.
That is 'til he heard me play.
Then he decided to ride along and listen.
It reminded him of home.  I puckered up
that Ol' Smokey all the way into town.
Then I arrested him.  Hell , I was the Sheriff
and he was a wanted man."*

# Harmonica Americana

## A Brief History

The year was 1865, the final year of the Civil War, and two boxes of crude ten-hole diatonic harmonicas were in the hull of a ship, making a jostling crossing from Germany to the United States. These small wooden and metal musical instruments were being sent here by the world's first true harmonica manufacturer, an ambitious young German clock maker by the name of Mathias Hohner. Very much a family affair, they'd been manufactured in the factory young Mathias ran with his wife and were to be unloaded at the dock by Hohner's immigrant cousins—then sold for the whoppin' price of ten cents apiece.

But would the guitar strumming, banjo picking, fiddle playing, tobacco spitting American public buy the new instrument? Flash forward a few months and imagine how much fun it must have been to witness the puzzled looks, smirks and catcalls as this new-fangled contraption called the "mouth organ" was displayed to American soldiers, farmers, cowboys, and townsfolk—probably by some guy with a thick German accent.

> *"What the heck you call that thang?"*
> *"You gonna make music out of that?"*

But when the foreigner started to play, well then, there'd be the sight of mouths dropping open, grins slowly spreading, and feet tapping as a whole world of music issued forth from the "furin' fella's" cupped hands.

> *"How much you say that doo-hickey cost?"*
> *"I'll take 'em all!"*

And that's how it all got started . . .

## The First Harmonica

Although it's less than two hundred years old, the harmonica is based on an ancient musical instrument— the sheng (Chinese for "sublime voice"), a mouth organ reputed to have been invented by Chinese Empress Nyu-kwa back in three thousand B.C. Like the harmonica, the sheng works as the player draws air in as well as blowing air out, and is capable of playing chords as well as single notes. These two characteristics mark the sheng and the harmonica unique among all of the world's wind instruments.

*The Sheng*

The reed used in the sheng and the harmonica is known as the "free-standing reed"—basically a sliver of wood or metal that's attached on one end, and left free to vibrate on the other. The pressure of moving air makes the free end vibrate, and a "sublime voice" is produced. The longer the reed, the lower the tone, and conversely, the shorter the reed, the higher the tone.

The ancient sheng came to Europe by way of a Jesuit missionary in the late 1700's. Around this time, an Irishman brought one from Russia. A Dane heard it being played and became fascinated with the idea of using the free-standing reed to mimic the sound of the human voice. He created a machine which said the words *mama* and *papa*—which understandably grew old pretty quickly. In 1792, a Russian by the name of Vogler put the free-standing reed in a pipe organ called the *orchestrion*. Although this unusual keyboard didn't become popular, it did spread awareness of the remarkable free-standing reed and its ability to produce tones previously unheard in European music.

## Buschmann's Aura

The man generally credited with the invention of the modern-times harmonica was actually a sixteen-year-old boy named Christian Friedrich Ludwig Buschmann. Around 1820, Christian put fifteen pitchpipes together and was delighted to find that he had created an instrument. He called it the *aura* and described it as "a truly unique musical instrument . . . only four inches in diameter and equally high, with twenty-one notes with piano and crescendo playing possibilities but without piano keys . . . with harmonies of six tones, which can be held as long as the player has breath."

It is said that in Vienna fashionable ladies took to wearing the *aura* as a pendant, and as an evening progressed they would lift it to their lips and play merry little tunes to keep their gentlemen friends entertained.

As clever as Buschmann's instrument was, it was quite different from the harmonica we play today. It was shaped more like a box than a harmonica, and had the disadvantage of being a blow-only instrument. Nonetheless, dozens of accomplished and would-be inventors took the idea and tried to expand upon it.

## The Vamper

In the 1820's a Bohemian inventor remembered only by his last name, Richter, came up with a crude prototype of the harmonica we play today. Richter gave his mouth organ a slender, framed shape you could cup in your hands, ten holes, and two reed plates—one for

*Vamper Harmonica, circa 1830. Protective plates were added in the 1880's. Note double hole arrangement for blows and draws.*

blowing and one for drawing. This meant a harmonica player could breathe in and out on one hole and each reversal of breath would produce a tone of a different pitch. He could then move to the next hole and play two different pitches, and the next hole after that. And because the player was breathing naturally—on the inhale and the exhale—there was no need to ever run out of breath!

As for the sequence of notes, Richter did something unusual. He created a wind instrument that, also like the sheng, could play both single notes and chords. The key to this was his unusual ordering of notes, leaving out some and doubling up on others. Using this vamp tuning (vamp is an old-fashioned musical term that means to improvise) one could play chords simply by making the mouth large enough to blow or draw several holes at one time. Single notes came from playing just one hole at a time.

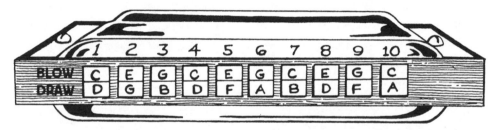

*The modern harmonica, this one in the key of C. If you blow on hole 1 you get a C note, draw and you get a D. Notice the missing notes of the scale on holes 2 and 3. The only complete scale starts at 4 blow. More on this later.*

This was ingenious! No matter where you put your mouth on the instrument, no matter whether you blew or sucked, because the notes were arranged in a side-by-side harmonizing sequence, you would be making harmonious, in-key and often surprising music!

Richter's success stimulated interest in the mouth organ, and in 1829 the first mass production began at a German clock factory. But about this time a depression struck Germany and Austria and many of the artisans were forced to look elsewhere for employment. Two of these, Christian Messner and Christian Weiss, began making harmonicas in their home workshop, and to them goes the credit of keeping our little harp alive through difficult times.

## Hohner Brings the Harmonica to America

It was the mid 1850's when the enterprising Hohner noticed the harmonica's potential and decided to try his hand at manufacturing. Learning his technique from Messner and Weiss (before they realized that he would become a competitor and stopped teaching him!) Hohner, his wife, and two employees produced six hundred and fifty harmonicas in his first year in business. The next year he produced more, and even more the year after that.

Seven years later, working on the notion that had taken over the world—that the future lay in America—the first boxes of Hohner harps were shipped to the shores of the USA. It's believed these Richter-tuned models were called "The Vamper."

Like the harmonica itself, nineteenth century American folk music was lyrical, but rowdy—sentimental, yet crude. It had Old World origins that had quickly become Americanized. When the easy-to-play, "sublime-toned," supremely portable harmonica added itself to the mix, performing the songs of the day, composing new ones, vamping the way an expert would on a fiddle or a guitar, it was as though a marriage had occurred—that of the harmonica and America.

Was the harmonica versatile? Man, it went everywhere. It played happy songs and lonesome songs. Played reels, jigs, breakdowns, waltzes, hymns, ballads, polkas, blues, field hollers, train sounds, lullabyes and broadsides. It calmed horses, wooed women, soothed hearts, won bets, stopped bullets, entertained children, told jokes, earned pennies and made good old manure-kicking music.

And it had this great tone! Tone you wouldn't believe. It could drum a rhythm like the hooves of horses or the chugging of a train. It could coo like the crying of a baby and just make sounds that let you feel good or made you sad. Overnight, it became the instrument of the drifter, the cowboy, the farmer, the field hand, railroad worker, the teacher, the soldier. It was used in minstrel shows, burlesque halls, churches and brothels—wherever and whenever the American people made music—which was everywhere and most all the time. By 1877, seventy per cent of Hohner's harmonica business was in the U.S. He had over two hundred employees and was producing over a million harmonicas a year. Not surprisingly, he was elected mayor of Trossingen—the quaint German village where the instruments were (and for the most part, still are) manufactured.

## Early American Harmonica Styles

In the early days, the harmonica was played in the style called Straight Harp, with the most important notes on the blow. This was, of course, the way the instrument had been designed to be played. If a harmonica was set in the key of C, the player played it in the key of C. If the harmonica was in the key of D, it was played in the key of D.

Moreover, the harpist would get individual notes by tongue-blocking—placing the tongue on the holes of the harmonica to block every hole except the one he wanted to play. He would then play that one hole for a single note and lift the tongue to play a chord. This alternation between single notes and chords produced an interesting "calliope" music, and an incredibly full effect.

During these early years, the harp took its place in the legends of the times. For instance, Jesse James's older brother Frank is said to have carried a harmonica in his pocket, which deflected a bullet, thereby ruining the harp but saving his life. It's also said that Wyatt Earp and Billy the Kid were harmonica players, that Daniel Boone made a bear dance with his harmonica (surely a bald-faced lie; the bear would want to play it!), that Davy Crockett played harmonica to the troops at the Alamo, and that Abe Lincoln brought a harmonica to the famous Lincoln-Douglas debates and said, "Mr. Douglas needs a brass band, but the harmonica will do for me!"

While the above probably contains more fiction than fact, old newspapers tell us that as early as the 1880's there were "French Harp" contests in barns and taverns throughout the South and Midwest. Historians speculate that it was during this time that the harmonica style called "Cross Harp" was developed. Cross Harp was a way of putting the accent on the draw notes of harmonica instead of the blow. Then, by changing the trajectory of the air coming through the harmonica into the mouth, the pitch and tone of the note could be "choked" or "bent" to actually lower the tone of the note. Because the harp player was playing the draw scale instead of the blow scale, the C harp would be played in the key of G. The D harp would be played in the key of A and so on.*

While Cross Harp was not the best for playing the songs of the day, it was tremendous for creating effects such as the driving rhythms of trains, the lonesome moan of the train whistle, and the huffing and puffing of fox and hound chases. It was also, with its warm and wailing tones, the best style for playing the musical sounds of the recently freed African-American slaves—the music that would one day be known as "the blues."

* This is explained more fully in Chapter Six.

## The Blues is Born

It all goes back to the incredible musical storytellers of Africa, known as *griots*. The *griots'* tales, passed generation to generation, were told in chants and songs. Drums were played, chorus repeated and to express strong feelings the griot would use a slurring vocalization known as the "falling tone."

When the Blacks were enslaved in America, many of the old stories and traditions were lost, but others were kept alive, and with them the techniques and styles so foreign to Western culture. One of the musical instruments the slaves brought with them was the banjo, based on a drumhead and string combo. Another was a hand-held mouth instrument called "the quill" which was quite adept at making that funky falling tone. When the harmonica invaded the South, it was natural for the quill-playing Blacks to switch over to it. It had more notes, and once you learned how to slur those low draw notes down, man, the falling tones (also known as "bent" notes) just rolled out.

At the turn of the century, hundreds, perhaps thousands, of black musicians travelled the roads of the South, living hard, playing hard, making their music for pennies, nickels and dimes—a music that combined the driving rhythms and falling tones of African music with the basic I-IV-V musical structure used by every western composer from Stephen Foster to Mozart.

This was the blues, a style of music that emerged from the most difficult and humble beginnings , and would one day pervade every facet of our popular musical culture. In his autobiography, *Father of the Blues,* black composer W.C. Handy claimed to first hear the blues played on a slide guitar in a train station in the late 1800's. "A loose limbed negro commenced plucking on a guitar while I slept. His feet were rags, his face had on it the sadness of the ages. As he played, he pressed a knife on the strings of the guitar in the manner popularized by Hawaiian guitarists. The effect was unforgettable . . . it was the weirdest music I had ever heard."

Of course the European Americans weren't ready for this "weird-ness" and the blues became what was known as "race music"—a separate "lower" music played on its own radio stations, recorded in its own recording studios, published by its own music publishing houses. A white man born in 1880 might go through his entire life and never hear the blues. Yet the blues—blues harmonica, blues singing, blues guitar—were there . . . and flourishing. It was played on sidewalks and in juke joints, radio stations and 78 rpm records. The musicians learned from each other and a rich tradition of music and blues songs soon developed.

Much of this tradition revolved around the great guitar players such as Blind Lemon Jefferson, Robert Johnson, Charlie Patton and their cohorts—those early geniuses of blues harmonica like Will Shade, Noah Lewis, George "Bullet" Williams, Sonny Boy (John Lee) Williamson I, Sonny Boy (Rice Miller) Williamson II, Rhythm Willie, Jazz Gillum. These guys played a rough, free-flowing Cross Harp blues. When they sang, their voices were raw, usually filled with pain and hard-living. Yet, like the story-telling of Africa, there was something eternal in their music.

One word of advice Sonny Boy Williamson II gave to his protegee, James Cotton, applies to us all. "Nothin' happens, boy, if you don't play your harp." What Sonny Boy was saying was, if you want to make music, if you want to have a good time, if you change your mood, or change the mood of others, don't sit around and wait for someone to do it for you. Pull out your music-maker and start blowing!

## The Country Tradition

In the early years, even before the advent of the blues, the har-monica shined in jug bands and stringed bands, as well as being a popular solo instrument. Both Cross Harp and Straight Harp styles were employed, and whites and blacks borrowed freely from each other. Bands travelled from town to town and harmonica players came from miles away to gather in barns and competitions. Most of these players were brought together by the clarion call of radio, for it was radio that brought news and music into the rural areas where country music was being forged.

It's in country music we see the remaining traces of the time when the songs in this book, the songs of **Harmonica Americana**, were the most popular. The fiddle was the mainstay instrument of this tradition and the harmonica player often tried to emulate the sounds of the country fiddler. Moreover, the early broadcasts of this time (among the most popular were "Grand Ol' Opry" and "National Barn Dance") frequently matched harmonica players with fiddlers.

Two of the early harp players who broadcast over the radio were Henry Whitter and Dr. Humphrey Bate. As brilliant as these gents were, neither got the exposure given our first true country harmonica star—a small hunchbacked black man by the name of Deford Bailey. Standing in front the huge radio microphone, little DeFord played train imitations, fox chases, melodies and blues on the Grand Ol' Opry, that famous radio show broadcast out of Nashville. His greatest hit was "Pan American Blues," an instrumental train imitation filled with effects that we today can only scratch our heads and wonder at. Deford died in Nashville in 1982.

Later, when radio became more commonplace and was broadcast out of almost every medium-sized burg in the country, harmonica players sometimes hosted shows in which they played, pitched products and even sold harmonicas. In the 1940's, broadcasting over KFFA radio in Helena, Arkansas, the gregarious blues player Sonny Boy Williamson II hosted his famous "King Biscuit Flour Hour,"—playing harmonica, selling the flour and sneaking in the details of where he was performing that night. Ten years later, Wayne Raney, the maestro of "hillbilly harp," sold more than one million "talking harmonicas" and instruction books over radio throughout the South. As for the other media, sometimes late at night you can still catch a movie from the 'thirties or 'forties with country players such as Lonnie Glosson, Jimmie Riddle, or Wayne Raney honking incredible hillbilly cross harp. But sadly, there are few photos, little documentation, and in most cases, only recordings, of the players before 1960.

## The Chromatics

There is an exception to this—and his name is Larry Adler, master of the chromatic harmonica. Back in Germany, the Hohner Harmonica Company continued to refine their popular instrument and create new instruments that were increasingly complex. The remarkable chromatic harmonica was developed in the 1920's and brought to America. It was the perfect instrument for a country that was getting interested in big band music and jazz. Unlike diatonic* harmonicas, chromatic harmonicas weren't set up with vamp tuning. They didn't play chords, and they couldn't bend notes. However, what chromatics could do was play all the notes of the scale, like a piano (Pushing in the slide gave you the black keys.) This dynamic instrument was to give rise to a revolution in harmonica playing.

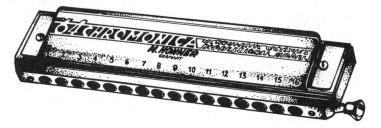

In the 1920's, 30's and 40's, Larry Adler's chromatic renditions of George Gershwin and other great composers thrilled the nation. His first commercial recording, "Smoke Gets in Your Eyes," sold two hundred thousand copies—an auspicious start to an illustrious career. For the last sixty years, Larry has composed for and played with symphonies, big bands, movies, and is considered one of the greatest musicians in the world. His very stardom as well as the rich, full-throated sound of his harp has inspired thousands to take up the instrument. To our government's disgrace, this innocent man was blackballed in the Hollywood Communist witch-hunt in the early 1950's, and at the time of this writing lives in London.

---

\* A five-dollar word that describes the basic eight-tone scale that goes *do re mi fa sol la ti do,* and corresponds to the white keys on the piano. The chromatic scale (with 12 tones) includes the black keys (the half-steps) and is more complex. See Chapter Six for more on this subject.

With the help of Adler and others, the harmonica scene moved away from the little diatonic instrument and into the world of the chromatic. Around this time, Jerry Murad's Harmonicats harmonica group had a huge hit with a song called "Peg O' My Heart." Harmonica bands sprung up across the country as Hohner came out with a variety of harps intended to suit the needs of a complete ensemble.

In a typical harmonica band, one player would play a blow-only bass harmonica, another, a chord harmonica. Another would solo . . . usually on a chromatic. The acts, some featuring as many as ten harmonica players at a time, were carefully orchestrated, presented in the vaudevillian tradition, and the music was stupendous. Along with The Harmonicats, we've had Borah Minevitch and the Harmonica Rascals, Johnny Puleo and his Harmonica Gang, Carl Freed and the Harmonica Harlequins, The Cappy Barra Harmonica Ensemble, Johnny O' Brien and the Harmonica Hi-Hats. Harmonica bands live on to this day, but one must seek these excellent musicians out. For more information, contact the S.P.A.H. organization, listed in the back of this book

## Modern Age Blues Harmonica

While mainstream America was grooving to Adler and the chromatics, the blues was trying on a new set of clothes: this time, city duds. During the thirties and the forties there was a huge migration of blacks from the rural South to the urban North (mostly Chicago) and with this change of landscape came a change of music. Under the guidance of slide guitarist Muddy Waters, the blues became amplified, driven by drums and electric guitar, and the blues harp was a mainstay in the band.

By 1950, the man generally considered the father of modern blues harp, "Little Walter" Jacobs had amplified his diatonic and chromatic harmonicas by cupping a radio microphone together with the harp in his hands. Playing through a guitar amplifier, he produced a warm, big-toned harp sound remarkably like that of a saxophone. Little Walter had a huge nationwide harmonica instrumental hit called "Juke" in 1952, but because it was race music it was unheard by most Americans.

Through the fifties, many other great blues players came into the forefront, but it's pretty well accepted that the "Big Five" are Sonny Terry (real name Saunders Terrell), who played a brilliant chord-based country blues, Jimmy Reed, a remarkable songwriter who played what might be called pop blues on the high end of his harp, the innovative "Little Walter" Jacobs who gave his harp that "saxophone sound," the smooth, jazzy and under-appreciated "Big Walter" Horton, and the incomparable Sonny Boy Williamson II who's included in both eras of blues harp players because he lived such a long time and influenced everyone.

These guys were incredible. Playing mostly diatonic harp, they fronted their own bands, singing in their rough gravelly voices, writing songs out of the scrap heap of American language, forging the modern blues from traditions born of Africa and the Deep South, in particular, the Mississippi Delta. Their music has become the bedrock of blues harmonica tradition, a style that now influences country western, rock n' roll, folk and jazz. The men who made this rich and vibrant music led unsheltered, often violent and whisky-soaked lives—lives we would consider tragic if their contributions had not been so great.

For example, Little Walter left his impoverished Georgia home at age seven, wandered the roads, learned the blues harp from the masters of the day, created a new style, and was stabbed to death in his thirty-sixth year in a Chicago bar. But he was only following tradition. Twenty years earlier, John Lee Williamson (Sonny Boy Williamson I) was murdered in a Chicago club. Less tragically, six foot four, two-hundred-and-fifty pound Sonny Boy Williamson II (a.k.a. "Rice Miller," "Little Boy Blue," "Footsie" "The Goat") stole Sonny Boy I's name, became famous with it, and in his late sixties toured England appearing with rock groups, dressed in the bowler and topcoat of an English gentleman, often carrying a half-imbibed fifth of whisky on stage with him. What a character! And, of course, the great Sonny Terry was blinded in one eye at age eight, the other when he was thirteen. A few years later, he took to the road, a blind youth playing harmonica for nickels and dimes, rambling from town to town with his unique, droning, hold-the-harmonica-up-side-down style. This great artist eventually played in Carnegie Hall.

Make no mistake. These men were giants—musical geniuses who were paid little for their contributions during their lifetimes, and when it came to trouble, they were tough as nails. One might guess their music was their only salvation. But what a salvation it was.

## After 100 Years

It was during the 1960's when the good old-fashioned ten-holed diatonic Vamper style harmonica took over where the chromatic had left off and became the number one harmonica in the country. And who did it? The kids . . . borrowing (or is that stealing?) from the old folks.

For example: Bob Dylan (a devotee of Woody Guthrie's hillbilly music), the Beatles' John Lennon (a musical genius/ rudimentary harmonica player who created his own style, neither blues nor hillbilly), Paul Butterfield (who played blues in the Little Walter vein), and English harpist John Mayall (a Sonny Boy II student who became a great innovator). Each of these players enjoyed tremendous popularity. Moreover, there was tasty harp on the Rolling Stones recordings (played by Brian Jones and Mick Jagger), an exciting country western player named Charlie McCoy who claimed Little Walter as his influence, and John Fogerty's hot licks as he "ran through the jungle" for Creedence Clearwater Revival. Suddenly it seemed the harp was everywhere, and everyone dug it.

Close your eyes and imagine Sonny Terry sitting on an old fruit box in front of a country grocery store and playing "Lost John" for nickels and dimes in 1936. Hear those lonesome sounds? See that distinctive hand flourish as he whoops, caterwauls, wails and warbles? Now flash forward thirty years and imagine thousands of kids in a huge stadium stomping their feet to the sight and sound of hippie-garbed, spike-haired Englishman John Mayall doing the same song. It was an old sound, but to the generation of the sixties raised on the musical politeness of Doris Day, Dean Martin, Patti Page, Johnnie Ray etc., it was a new sound, and, man, it was thrilling. By 1966, harmonica sales in the United States had skyrocketed as more and more people (mostly kids, like me, who wanted to be Dylan, Lennon, Butterfield or Mayall) puckered up and got hooked on harp. It became an attitude, an attitude that loved harp, loved authenticity, loved American music—an attitude I call **Harmonica Americana.**

And it's still going strong.

## Into the Nineties

Many of those kids who were so inspired by the great players of yesterday got really good themselves. In fact, one could say that today's harp players, while maybe not as colorful as Sonny Boy and Little Walter, are better than ever. A complete list would be exhaustive, but for anyone who wishes to investigate contemporary harmonica music, you should definitely check out the following players because they are great. In the country western field are Mickey Raphael (who plays for Willie Nelson), P.T. Gazell, Don Brooks, Charlie McCoy (his "Orange Blossom Special" is a classic) and Terry McMillan.

In blues and rock, listen to Kim Wilson (of the Fabulous Thunderbirds), Phil Wiggins, Rick Estrin (of Little Charlie and the Nightcats), Junior Wells, Al Wilson (now twenty years deceased, of Canned Heat), Charlie Musslewhite, John Mayall, Rod Piazza, Paul Butterfield, Tom Ball, Bill Tarsha, John Popper, Mark Hummel, Jerry Portnoy, William Clarke, Paul deLay, James Cotton, James Harman, Magic Dick (of the J. Geils Band) Carey Bell and the incredible "Madcat" Ruth. Following the blues harp tradition set by the "Big Five," (whose recordings you should also listen to) most of these players are also singers and front their own blues bands. Be sure to check them out, either in concert or recording.

As for folk music, listen to guitar wizard Doc Watson play harp, because he's one of the best around. Like Bob Dylan, Bruce Springsteen, Utah Phillips, Donovan, Neil Young, Woody Guthrie and countless other troubadours of note, Doc puts his harp in a "rack" so he can play guitar and harp at the same time. (It's interesting to note that these harp and guitar specialists are among the most influential players we've ever had.) For those who wonder why Dylan is so important, the best example of what he can do to a harp is on his first album, called "Bob Dylan." Wild, rugged and gritty, "Bob Dylan" is a masterpiece of country Straight Harp plus impassioned singing, yodeling, guitar playing and good old-fashioned, raw-boned musicality.

In a category which is neither blues, folk or country are Norton Buffalo, Howard Levy (who has truly taken the diatonic harmonica further than anyone else) and Lee Oskar. These are three of our best.

Session men are also great harpists. These are the players of the harmonica music you hear on television shows and in radio commercials. Once you listen for it, you'll be amazed at how much harmonica there is—from Levi commercials (Tom Ball) to the Rosanne show (Juke Logan) to McDonald commercials (Tommy Morgan).

Not to be slighted are the chromatic men, masters of jazz, classical and pop. These include Jean "Toots" Thielemans, Charles Leighton, Tommy Reilly, Robert Bonfigliano, Eddy Manson, Blackie Shackner, William Galison, Stevie Wonder, Larry Adler, and Richard Hayman. Toots is often cited as the greatest of them all but it was Adler who riveted generations of music-lovers (including yours truly at the age of three) and is considered the grandfather of the chromatic harp.

You can acquire recordings of almost all the players listed here from the sources listed in the back of this book.

## The Harp and You

Whew! Just writing about these great players, past and present, makes me want to pick up my harp and play it. Before I do, I have one more thought about the harmonica and its history. Probably each of us has a memory of someone who has musically brightened an afternoon or an evening, a campfire or a car ride, with sweet harmonica sounds—their eyes closed, hands fluttering, body swaying. Or perhaps you can recall a movie that made you cry, with the harmonica providing the music. Or the time you heard someone who was really hot, and just could not believe the sound that came out of that little baby.

Maybe it was a grandparent or parent who made this memory for you. Or a stranger who unwittingly provided a harmonica soundtrack to some now-distant time in your life. Perhaps someone gave you a harmonica when you were a child and it was you who played, and now you'd like to try again. This is the other history, the history of your life and the harmonica somehow intertwined, the truest and most meaningful history of the little harp—and we all share it.

You see, the harmonica is a part of who we are. It's the instrument of *our* culture, yours and mine. Each note sings of German tinkerers in a small town, American slaves crying their pain and loneliness, cowboys sighing about their far-away love, city folks trumpeting the jazz and glory of neon-lit mean streets, and folks like you and me celebrating the everyday joys of life and living. It is truly an instrument of the heart and soul.

And that's why I play it.

\* For a comprehensive history of the harmonica and its great players, see these two excellent books: *Harmonicas, Harps and Heavy Breathers,* by Kim Field, published by Simon & Schuster and *The Harp Handbook* by Steve Baker, published by Louis Hermann Demmler.

# Chapter Two

# Vamping the Harp to the Sweet Flow of Music

*"I'll never forget the time Billy Makeshift and I went down that old Comstock mine with our picks and shovels. We kept going deeper into the cool, damp darkness until we could make out some music echoing up the shaft. Billy kept saying he wanted to dance with me, but what the hell, he was drunk. Finally we came across this big bearded fellow playing "Oh! Susannah" on his mouth organ with one hand as he swung his pick with the other. Tell you one thing. That man was strong. Tell you something else. He made pretty good music on that little harmonica. Yesiree, the harmonica was the instrument for him. He played the rest of the afternoon, swinging his pick and blowing that tin sandwich. That's the day I started playing it too."*

# Your Natural Talent . . .

*You* are musical. In fact, *everyone* is musical. It's part of being a human being, part of being alive. Months before you were born, your forming cells danced to the bass drum of your mother's heart, the whoosh of blood in her veins, the steady sound of her breathing. This is how you grew arms, legs, feet and brain—to the *sound* of music. Although you may not remember those magic days of early childhood, you most certainly sang up a storm, becoming a master at *twinkle twinkle*, *baa baa black sheep* and a few compositions of your own.

Growing older you grooved to the music of your time, danced to it, sang it, fell in love to it, and like everyone else were just generally moved, motivated, entertained and persuaded by it. Even now, as you read these words, your body is making the music that keeps you alive; in the rhythm of your breathing and the pulse of your heartbeat.

You see, like all of us, there's music in your memory, your emotions, and music in your heart. That's probably why you've got this book in your hands right now—you're musical and you want to express it. As a teacher of thousands of burgeoning harp players, this is what I've discovered: there is a well-spring of musical talent in each of us.

But there are enemies to your natural talent and you might as well know who they are. Let's say you had a strict, demanding music teacher when you were a child, or there were people who made fun of you when you tried to sing. Today, when you start to play, these experiences live on as critical voices in your head. "That's not good enough!" "You aren't musical!" "Who are you trying to kid?" Sound familiar? How can you or anyone else learn to play when there's an imaginary chorus of nitpickers shouting you down or sucking away your motivation whenever you pick up your instrument to play?

For many people, the first step is to soften those critical voices. So, as your teacher, I want to make a deal with you. When you hear those nattering nabobs of negativity, tell 'em to shut up. Then replace those negative words with affirmative words that help you learn. " Hey, I sound pretty good." "I'm off to a good start!" "I'm gonna be great!" and even "I'm great!"

Another thing that will help soften those critical voices—let your fantasies run wild. Maybe that's you sitting up there in that drawing up above, blowing some sweet harmonica sounds with a couple of good old boys from fifty years ago. Maybe that's you on the radio playing with Garth or Randy, B.B. King or the Beatles. For that matter, maybe that's you on the stage, cupping that microphone to your harp, down on one knee, just wailing.

So remember, you *do* have natural talent. You *do* have the right to make music. And you can learn to play. Our deal? You're going to give yourself positive reinforcement as I give you the information and the program. It's going to be fun. It's going to be simple. And it's going to happen day-by-day and step-by-step. So come on, let's make sure you've got the right kind of harp and get started with some easy first sounds.

# What Kind of Harmonica?

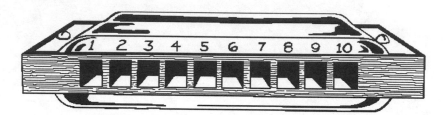

*Introducing the one, the only, the incredible, amazing, phenomenal, sweet-sounding, eternally popular, musically transcendent…ten-holed mouth organ.*

In my opinion the basic 10-hole garden-variety diatonic harp is the best one for playing the songs of **Harmonica Americana**. This is the harmonica that gets that expressive *wa wa* sound. The kinds I recommend average about twenty-five dollars for the best, six dollars for the budget model.

Some of these are:

**"Pocket Pal"** an inexpensive starter harp that usually comes with instructional kits. A little bit more difficult to play than the harps described below, but just fine for a trial run.

**"Special 20"** a plastic combed, tightly constructed, moderately priced professional harp. One of my favorites.

**"Big River"** a new and slightly less-expensive harmonica with bright tone and quick response. Great for beginners and intermediate players.

**"Marine Band"** designed in 1896 for John Phillip Sousa's Marine Band. This is the legendary blues harp with wooden comb and warm sound. I learned on it—today I find it more difficult to play, but lots of folks won't play anything else.

**"Lee Oskar"** an easy-playing harp with bright tone and slightly larger holes. The "Oskie" was designed by Lee himself, one of our best players.

But that's just a start. There are over fifty models of diatonic harps. While the different models *do* create a difference in tone and feeling, it's *single note technique* that matters in determining sound, not the model of harmonica. An exception: try a double-reeded, tremolo-tuned or octave-tuned **Echo Harp.** While you lose that distinctive *wa wa* quality, the beautiful echoes give you an old-timey "Christmas" tone that could be perfect for many of the songs you'll be learning.

You can also use a **chromatic harmonica** to play the songs of **Harmonica Americana.** You'll lose that wonderful *wa wa,* and you won't be able to play chords, but because the chromatic has *all* the notes of the scale, you'll avoid that pesky problem of missing notes that plagues us diatonic lovers.

## Your Ol' Buddy

When you've gotten into buying some harps, you'll notice that one little baby has a particular sound, soul or feeling to hold or play that no other harp has. This could be a Pocket Pal, or it could be a Special 20. The model doesn't seem to matter. What does matter is a subtle thing that's hard to describe. The tone. The bend. The way blowing it makes you feel. This is the harp you keep for a long time. The harp you keep in a special box. The harp you give a name to. When you buy a new harmonica you never know if you're buying this special harp, or if you're getting one that's like any other.

## What About My Old Harmonica?

Let's say you have an old harp that's been rattling around your drawer for the last twenty years. Should you get a new one? It all depends. It could be that special one. Then again it could be an old clunker that's going to make learning impossible. What's important is that your harmonica plays, that the reeds don't rattle, that the major holes (1 through 8) all work, that the plates aren't bent or rusty, that it's reasonably clean, and that it feels good to play. If your old harp doesn't qualify, replace it. (Keep old harps in your glove box, saddlebag or briefcase to use as a back-up.)

## Is This Harmonica Broken?

Folks just starting out frequently have trouble with the low draw notes—in particular 2 and 3 draw. Getting a sound on holes 8, 9 and 10 can also be troublesome. If these are problem holes for you, it's probably your technique, not a defective harp. As you read this book, you'll learn how to get beautiful tone out of all the holes of your harmonica. On the other hand, you may want to . . .

## Buy A New Harmonica

When it comes to replacing your harmonica, or buying many harps in different keys , I say—do it. Get yourself a brand-spanking-new "Special 20" or "Lee Oskar." Treat yourself to a "Golden Melody" or a "Big River." Even though the prices on harmonicas have increased the last twenty years, they're still the best buy in the music store. We're talking about a lifetime of music for twenty to thirty bucks. Where can you get a better bargain? (Of course, over time you'll own more than one harmonica.)

## What Key Is This Harmonica In?

There's a letter printed on the end of your harmonica: **your harp's key.** You can buy harmonicas in any of the twelve musical keys and each is identical—they simply play higher or lower. For instance, G is the lowest key of harp, F sharp is the highest and C is in the middle. You can play the same song in exactly the same way, on exactly the same holes, on any of these keys of harp. The F sharp version will be high, the A flat version will be low, and the C harp (which is probably the one you own) will sound out between the two.

Although the trusty C harp is a great place to start, before long you'll own harps in all keys. This adds variety and lets you accompany guitarists and singers who may be playing in different keys. The most common keys are A, C, D, E, F and G. There's a special quality to the E flat and D flat harps, so get these too.

## A Few Words on Keeping Your Harps Nice

There are only a few rules of beginning harp maintenance and most of them are of the common sense variety. Warm your harps up by playing them softly before you go full tilt. Don't play with food, drink or smoke in your mouth. In fact, gargle water to wash your mouth out. Put your harps in their boxes when you're through playing.

Tap the saliva out of the harp between songs. Between practice sessions, use a toothpick or tooth-brush to clean the gunk out of the corners of the harp holes. Tilt the harp down so the gunk doesn't fall in the hole.

As I mentioned, lots of times the 2 draw and 3 draw notes don't seem to respond properly. This is usually due to faulty technique, not a broken harmonica. Use the suggestions on pages 66 and 138-141 to work on proper technique and you'll get those notes humming.

On the other hand, when a *blow* note goes bad, there's usually a problem with your instrument. This might be a beard or mustache hair, food or dried gunk stuck in a reed. First, try blowing and drawing a little harder on that hole to free the reed. If that doesn't work, run the harp under a tap for moment and shake the water out. If that doesn't work, use a small screw driver to remove the plates so you can get to the reeds and gently get the hair out of there. No good ever came from sticking the screwdriver directly into the hole.

A harp will go bad once in a while when it's not your fault. In the case of the Hohner instruments, there's a guarantee, so you can return the instrument. Be sure to tell them what the problem is. But consider this, repairs and shipping take awhile. It's also possible that the repair department will point out that the problem was your error, not a problem in quality control. What can a harp player do? In the case of the "Lee Oskar" harps, you can buy a new reed plate. Not cheap, but better than having to buy a whole new Oskie. How long do harps last? Depends how hard you play, how often you play, and how you keep them. So let's put it this way— they don't last forever, but they last long enough. And luckily, they're not too expensive to replace.

# Doc Gindick's Ten Suggestions for Great Harmonica Tone

1. Although the harmonica should be deep in your mouth, your lips should be really loose—barely touching the upper and lower plates of the instrument.

2. When you draw, feel as though you are inhaling some of the air through your nose.

3. Don't blow and draw by taking huge breaths from your lungs. Instead breathe easily, shallowly, and avoid running out of breath. (See the section on breathing)

4. If you do start to get winded, try cutting in half the amount of air you blow and draw through the harp.

5. Strive for fluidity of sounds. Avoid choppiness and gaps of silence.

6. Avoid making blatting sounds. Instead, make your sounds start softly, get louder, and then trail off a bit.

7. Try clenching the harmonica between your teeth as you blow and draw (look Ma, no hands!) and see if it improves your sound. Then take the harmonica out of your teeth, put it back between your relaxed lips and try to get the same quality of tone.

8. To help yourself get a closer feel for the harp, try closing your eyes as you explore. (Not recommended while driving.)

9. The next step is to slide the harmonica in your mouth as you blow and draw, making some sounds long and some short.

10. Really **listen** to your harmonica. One way to sharpen your hearing ability is cup a hand behind one ear as you play. (This is a technique singers use.) Now, experiment and make that little harp sing sweet and pretty.

# First Sounds

First, say hello to your harp. If you want to give it a name—say, Herman, Schatzie, Bernice—I won't tell anybody. Now, hold that little sweetness with its numbers facing up. Your fingers should be curved in a natural position well away from the numbers and the holes they identify. Avoid pointing your elbows out so they flap like the wings of a chicken. Instead, tuck them comfortably in towards your body. And most important, relax . . .

*RELAX...*

Ready? Bring the harp into your mouth so holes 1, 2 and 3 are very lightly covered with your lips. I know that once you get the harp in your mouth you can't see the numbers, so just do your best. In fact, to be sure you're getting hole number 1 along with the others, tuck the end of your harp into the corner of your lips.

Now, blow *very* gently and make your blow last about 5 seconds. Hear that sound? This is a chord (a combination of notes that harmonize together) I call this chord **123 blow** because these are the holes you're playing. Spend some time working on getting that pretty, smooth sound. First rule: no big blasts of air. It's O.K. if your teeth are touching the harmonica In fact, this might help. Second rule: no tight mouth. *Really* relax your lips, jaw, throat, nose, tongue, stomach—everything. (One way to relax your face is to scrunch everything up, then let it all go flaccid.)

Now try a draw (polite for "suck"). Keep those lips loose—barely touching the harmonica! Again, it's O.K. for the harp to touch the teeth. Draws are more difficult than blows and require a lighter touch. No loud blats, honks, horks or foghorns. Keep a soft mouth and relaxed jaw and throat. Go back and forth between the draws and blows. Experiment. Easy does it. Hey! You sound pretty good!

# Harmonica Wild!

This is your harmonica childhood. Time to take advantage of the harp being one of the easiest instruments in the world to improvise on. That's why they call it "the Vamper." So go for it. Be wild and wooly, soft and tender. Make the harmonica sad, happy, bored, yearning, begging. (All you have to do is think of these feelings as you play.) Blow, draw, slide, tongue, change mouth size and shape. In short, just hang out with your harp and see what happens. You can spend days doing this. Heck, some people spend years. I call this . . .

## Cowboy Style Harmonica

Don't worry about making music so much as creating a mood. Make it a cowboy-campfire-horseback-lonesome-but-happy mood. Don't be afraid to be corny or dramatic. Music *is* drama. To end your lonesome song about life on the prairies, make your mouth wide and blow holes 4,5,6 and 7 at the same time. This chord (called the Big Blow Chord) will give your random sounds a feeling of resolution. More on this later.

## Borrow-a-Song

Another way to make your random wanderings sound like a song is to pretend you *are* playing a song. Anything from "The Sound of Music" to "Yodeling Jack and The Cowgirl's Purple Boots" (One of my favorites). Even though the notes and the song you come up with will probably be very different than the song you're using for inspiration, you'll be using the music in your memory and the tongued cadence of the lyrics to put a musical feeling (rhythm and phrasing) into these early sounds. But forget this fancy music-talk. Borrow a song and rustle-up some music.

* You can also play cowboy style on the songs of Harmonica Americana by playing two or more notes at a time instead of single notes. This is also sometimes called the "Close-Enough" style.

# Tonguing That Talking Sound

*"Listen to the harp player's rhythm! He makes it sound like he's playin' a mile a minute! Yet he's calm and relaxed, like he's hardly workin'. Makes me wanna dance. How's he do that?"*

Now that you're blowing and drawing gentle, sweet-sounding chords, let's try **tonguing**—a very important technique that effortlessly stops and starts the voice of your harmonica without you having to stop and start your breath.

Here's how it works. **Say "ta."** Feel where the tip of your tongue strikes the fleshy ridge behind your upper teeth? This is exactly the move you make with your tongue to break up your notes, and create syllables in your sounds. Now put the harp in your mouth and give this a try. Gently blow the center holes, say 4 and 5 blow, and tap your tongue to create three syllables. "Ta ta ta."

Remember: Don't stop your breath to create these syllables. Instead, keep your breath going and trust your tongue to do the work for you.

For example, as you gently blow into any of the middle or low holes on your harp you might tongue the rhythm and cadence of the words, *"I love my baby."* Notice how this gives the harp a diction, a language of its own. Try it a few times. Make that harp sing. "Ta ta ta ta ta."

Next, you might want to draw and tongue the syllables to the words, *"She keeps me satisfied."* You could go on all day doing this, drawing and blowing, moving the harp and tonguing the syllables of lyrics that pop into your head. *"I sent my rent check to my landlord. Hope it makes it there on time. My wife is pretty. Hope she likes my harp playing. Ta ta ta ta ta!"*

## Take Your Harp Somewhere Beautiful

My favorites are the sandy banks of slow-moving rivers and convenient overlooks on far-flung mountain trails. To my way of thinking, there's nothing more exhilarating than looking across the some grand mountain range and trying to express those larger-than-life feelings on my little harmonica.  And of course, at night, sitting around a campfire, nothing goes better than cowboy music and starlight.  So go ahead, take that little harp out into nature (even the back yard is nice) and make some sweet natural sounds.

# Chapter Three

# Blows, Draws and Balderdash

## Put Some Method in your Madness

*"It was back in 1878 I married that curly-haired
little Bernice Hudson out of Deadwood and
moved her down to my operation in the Silverado.
Truth be told, she couldn't cook or sew.
She didn't want to clean house, chop wood or
keep the ponies fed. What Bernice could do was play
"Turkey in the Straw" on the mouth organ.
She could play it forwards and backwards, double
time and triple time. She could turn that song on
its head and send it spinnin', and I guess that's why
I married her. Later on she became a school teacher,
and she learned a couple of more songs. Maybe
those two extra songs is why we're still married . . .
though learning to cook didn't hurt much either."*

# That Sweet Spot Right in the Middle

*"Seems like no matter where I go on the harmonica—blowin', drawin', goin' fast or slow, climbin' up the notes like a ladder and goin' back down again—it all sounds fine if I end up by blowin' that sweet spot right in the middle."*

Now for a little bit of theory that should help your cowboy music come off more like a real song instead of just random sounds—and if you don't get it, don't sweat it. It'll all make sense in due time. That said, here we go . . . **On a C harp, when you make your mouth wide and gently blow holes 4, 5, 6, and 7 at the same time (in fact, you can even throw in the 3 blow), you play a C Major chord. This is the Big Blow Chord and is the natural ending place for most of your impromptu cowboy-style songs.**

This is true of all the different keys of harmonica. If you were playing a D harp, 4567 blow would be a D chord. And if you were playing a G harp, 4567 blow would be a G chord. On any key of harmonica, when you let the Big Blow Chord be the foundation of your music, you're playing the style of harmonica called "Straight Harp." Straight Harp is the melodic style of harmonica—the style of most of the songs notated in this book.

And here's some good news. You can also produce the Straight Harp Blow Chord on **1234 blow** or **789 and 10 blow.** Think of it this way: a blow chord on the bottom, the middle or the top gives you the foundation for beginning harp music. And that, of course, is one reason the harmonica is so easy to learn to play. Right now, play up and down your harmonica, blowing, drawing and experimenting. To end your musical masterpiece of the prairies, play a long, fading 4567 blow. That's the Big Blow Chord.

* Straight Harp is also called 1st Position. As explained later, there are several possible positions on harmonica. Straight Harp is the most direct and best for playing the songs of Harmonica Americana.

# Structure, Scales, etc.

Here's a few facts to help you navigate your way around the harp:

- From holes 1 through 6, the blow sound is lower than the draw sound. On hole 7 and above, the draw is lower than the blow.

- The scale is the favorite of music teachers everywhere and gives you an idea of how the harp is laid out. There's only one complete major *do re mi* scale on the little diatonic harp. It starts on the 4 blow. Give it a try.

| 4 | ④ | 5 | ⑤ | 6 | ⑥ | ⑦ | 7 | |
|---|---|---|---|---|---|---|---|---|
| do | re | mi | fa | sol | la | ti | do | circled numbers mean draw |

| 7 | ⑦ | ⑥ | 6 | ⑤ | 5 | ④ | 4 | |
|---|---|---|---|---|---|---|---|---|
| do | ti | la | sol | fa | mi | re | do | uncircled mean blow |

- On a C harmonica, this is a C Scale. On a D harmonica, it's a D scale. Same rule applies to all keys of harps.

- If you try to play a scale on the low end of your harp, from 1 blow, you'll notice that the notes for *fa* and the *la* are missing. The only way to overcome this is to learn to "bend" notes—a way of changing your airstream and lowering the tone of the note. Bending is covered in the final section of this book for good reason: it's hard.

- I'll say it again: when you play your C harmonica in the key of C, emphasizing the blow sounds, and using the above scale as your musical framework, you are playing Straight Harp. It's the best way to play harmonica melodies.

- You impatient, tell-me-more, music-major types might ask, "Where are the individual C notes on the C harp?" The answer is: 1 blow, 4 blow, 7 blow and 10 blow (see page 17). These notes provide a natural starting and ending place for your harmonica songs. Browsing at the notation of the songs starting in Chapter Five, notice how all the melodies end on 4 blow or 7 blow. These are the root notes. As you blow and draw your way around the harmonica, try ending your songs on holes 4 or 7 blow.

# That Inner Beat

Rhythm comes from everywhere—the tapping of your foot, the rapping of a knuckle on a table top, pounding a fist into your palm, hammering a nail, listening to and watching your windshield wipers as they slosh back and forth across your windshield. The beat can be the constant clickity-clack of a freight train or the cloppity-clip of horses' hooves. Yes, the beat is here, there, everywhere. Breathing is beat. Heartbeat is beat. Life is beat. Now, let's put the beat into *your* music . . .

## 4/4 Time

One of the best beats to play harp to is the one you get by counting **1**-2-3-4-**1**-2-3-4 with the accent on the "1." **This is called 4/4 time**. It can be a fast 4/4 (such as "Turkey in the Straw") or a slow one (like a slow blues). Played fast, 4/4 time generally makes you want to bounce up and down and is good for dancing, marching etc.

## 3/4 Time

Another rhythm, in fact, the beat most of the songs in this book are set to, is the one you get by counting **1**-2-3-**1**-2-3-**1**-2-3 with the accent on the "1." **This is called 3/4 time or "waltz time."** It makes you want to sway back and forth and is known for its soothing, relaxing effect.  To feel this rhythm right now, count aloud "1-2-3-1-2-3" with the accent on the "1."

Now the songs of **Harmonica Americana** are presented with a time signature that tells you whether the music is in 3/4 or 4/4. But you might not need this. Just play the song in the rhythm that you know it to be. For instance, if you start playing "On Top of Old Smokey" the same way you've always sung it, you'll automatically be playing in 3/4 time.

The main point—Get into the habit of tapping your foot and bringing a strong sense of beat into your music. Remember: if there ain't no beat, there ain't no music!

# How's This Thing Work?

*blow*

At first glance, the harp is real simple. Inside each hole or chamber are two reeds, one on the top, one on the bottom. The reed on the top vibrates when air is **blown** through the chamber. The reed on the bottom vibrates when air is **drawn** through it.

*draw*

These vibrations, and the way they are created by your breath, mouth, tongue, hands and soul, create the sound that comes out of the harp. That's why it's important to pay attention as you try to get your harp to sing. The smallest change can make a big difference.

## About The Reeds

These guys and gals are thin strips of metal, fastened on one end, standing free on the other. If you were to pluck one of the longer ones, it would go *boing!* When you blow on it (or draw) it makes a sound. The longer the reed, the lower the sound. Going up the scale, the reeds get shorter as the notes get higher. The lower notes are produced by slower vibrations, higher notes by faster vibrations. Every reed's a little different. Some are problem children. Others are straight A students. You'll soon know which is which.

## Reeds, Vibrations, and Sounds

Imagine for a moment that you're a free-standing reed in a harmonica. What kind of airstream would make you hum to your hearts content? As you fool around on your harp, notice how changing your airstream and the shape of your mouth, throat etc. changes the tone of your harmonica sound.

Example: as you blow and draw on your harmonica, change your throat as though mouthing the vowel sounds: *A, E, I, O, U.* Notice how changing your throat and mouth changes the voice of the harmonica. Are there one or two throat-positions that produce tones you like better than others? I find *O* and *U* to be rounder and more expressive than the other positions. What's your opinion?

# Should You Get Serious About Harp?

As I close out this chapter of wonderfully easy harmonica instruction, I respectfully pose the above question for your consideration. Of course, you'll have to answer it for yourself, but I want to assure you that, like everything else in life, you'll get out of the harmonica what you put into it.

On the other hand, unlike everything else in life, you can have a great time each step of the way, and it won't cost you a bundle. As a matter of fact, once you've bought the damned thing, playing it is free.

So, if you're willing to spend some time with your instrument every day, to accept new challenges, and to believe in yourself as a musician, I say yes, get serious about harp. And enjoy every moment of it—because the point of all this work is to have fun.

On the other hand, be prepared for some frustration, because the better you get, the better you'll want to be. (At least, that's my experience.) It can become an addiction. You'll want to play all the time.

Now I know you're probably saying, "All I want to do is play Ol' Smokey' in front of a campfire!" Trust me. After you've done this, you'll want to do more, and more after that. The harmonica is a never-ending world that gradually becomes a way of life. This book will prove it to you.

Learning can be hard and frustrating. It's also one of life's greatest rewards. Just imagine how wonderful that campfire's going to feel with you playing a complete repertoire of great songs, people clapping, laughing, and singing to your music. Imagine jamming with other instruments, a group of you playing for friends, even making money! Should you get serious about the harp? Should you?

# Chapter Four

# Arts of the Harp

Mastering those special skills that make the harmonica
"the most beautiful instrument in the world."

*"There was this time in that Colorado saloon.
I think it was Em's or Emmy's or something
like that. I'd been doing a lot of practicing
out by myself and now this guitar-playin' farm boy
and myself got into this damned duet
on "Frankie and Johnny." As we moved into
"Turkey in the Straw," all the bargirls and
gamblers and cowboys started shouting out verses
and clapping their hands in time.
I couldn't believe how good I was playing!
Neither could they. "Beautiful Dreamer" was lovely
until someone bounced a glass off my head."*

# Playing Perfect Single Notes

CONCENTRATE...

*"Listen to that tone! Man, it reaches right through my chest into my heart. Sounds like a saxophone! Nope, sounds like a violin. Sounds like the human voice. Wrong! It sounds like a harmonica being correctly played . . ."*

So far we've been working on the easier part of harp playing—blowing, drawing, and basically just clowning around. Now I want to show you how to play that harp with unspeakably beautiful tone. You may find you need to stop yourself, to slow down and get patient in order to learn this. Believe me, it's worth it.

Playing a single note means **playing one note at a time in such a way that the note is clear, unimpeded, and ringing out rich and full.** This is the most important skill of harmonica playing, the basis of your own unique sound, **the foundation of everything more advanced.**

When you're just starting out, the best way to do it is by **puckering**—pushing your lips out well over the plates of the harmonica, tilting the back of the harmonica slightly up, and directing a gentle stream of air into the hole you're trying to play. The goal? Rich clear tone, and a really comfortable feeling as you produce it.

The first note to try is 4 blow. Obviously, you need to push your lips out and place the harmonica between them in such a way that neither the 3 blow or the 5 blow gets any air. As such, there's a tendency to be overly cautious and form a tiny whistle-hole that comes limping into that fourth hole. Wrong! Be bold! Embrace that 4 blow in a sensuous pucker. Push those lips out like the fat part of a big kiss!

A couple of Doc's rules are:

The **larger** your single note hole (but still being narrow enough to allow you to play one note at a time), the better your tone will be.

The **further** into your puckered lips you can place the harmonica, the better your tone will be.

Placing the harp on the edge of your lips guarantees thin, hissy tone and that takes all the pleasure out of your harp music. (Read the above at least three times . . . a day.)

So give it a try right now: Look at hole 4. Say to that hole, "I'm going to bring you to my mouth, push my lips into a perfect pucker, and gently blow a strong, clear single note."

Now, with a controlled stream of air that lasts about six seconds . . . calmly, carefully do it. Again. And again. And again.

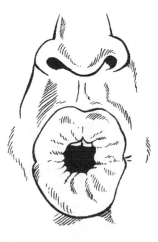

*Remember the goal is rich, pure tone, and the best way to get it is to truly relax your lips and face.*

*Don't be shy! When in doubt, pucker more . . . and place the harmonica deep within those puckered lips.*

# Doc Gindick's Surefire Take-Your-Time-and-Be-Patient Single Note Suggestions

1. Make your face, lips, throat as **relaxed** as possible as you pucker. One good way is to tighten them up and let them go limp several times.

2. **Make your single note opening higher than it is wide** (a vertical oval). Accomplish this by pushing your lips out, slightly dropping your jaw, and drawing the insides of your cheeks in towards your teeth.

3. Get your upper lip at least half-way over the top plate of the harmonica. An easy way to do this is to tilt the **back of the harmonica up.** This automatically gets the harmonica deeper into your mouth.

4. Try to make the **line between your nose and your upper lip curve out and up rather than down.** Again, you do this by puckering. Sometimes it helps to lift the harmonica (and your puckered mouthpiece) **up** towards your nose.

5. Avoid puffing your cheeks as you blow and draw. Instead, **focus the air into a narrow channel.** Sometimes it helps to push from your stomach.

6. If you hear two notes instead of one, **try sliding the harp a bit to the left or right** to help you "lock" onto the note.

7. Avoid giving the harp a short toot, taking it out of your mouth, glaring at it, and then trying it again. Instead, **play long, controlled streams of air,** and slowly and subtly change your approach until your single note rings through.

8. If my suggestions don't work for you, take another look at that hole, concentrate, and do it **your** way. Then over a period of time, improve your tone by moving slowly in the direction of my suggestions.

# Single Note Do's and Don'ts

### Two examples of correct technique

Try tilting the
harmonica up

Notice line between
nose and lip.  It's relaxed.

### Two common mistakes

Stiff upper lip.  Harmonica on edge of lips.  Guarantees bad tone.

# Control and Focus

## That Single Note Airstream

As you work on getting a single note, put the words **control** and **focus** in the front of your mind.

Here's an example of what the phrase *control and focus* means: When blowing a soap bubble from a plastic ring, you carefully manipulate the airstream coming from your mouth so the bubble can form in the ring. You control and focus the air, right? This is the same thing you do when you play a single note. You place the harp deep between your puckered lips and instead of *watching* the bubble to adjust your airstream, you *listen* to the sound of the harmonica. Then you carefully adjust.

Are you getting that slightly blurry chord sound of two notes side by side playing at the same time? Control, focus and *narrow* the airstream. That's right, push your lips from the inside out and concentrate. Sometimes it helps to practice in front of a mirror. Sometimes it helps to turn off all the lights, sit in a comfortable chair, and get very quiet and attentive to your little friend, the harp. Sometimes it helps to imagine hearing the sound of the note you're try to play, and then to play it.

What *always* helps is to concentrate.

## Tune in Like a Radio

A student of mine said learning to play a single note is like tuning in a radio station on an old fashioned radio. You keep adjusting the dial until the thing locks in. When learning to play a single note, keep adjusting the harp, sliding to the left and the right, *and* keep on blowing or drawing so you have *something to hear* until the note locks in.

# Anatomy of a Single Note Pucker

Flesh between nose and lip
curved up and out.

Important! Harmonica
deep within
puckered lips.

Back of harp tilted up.

Corners of lips pulled in,
as though you were
about to gently bite
insides of cheeks.

Face is relaxed.

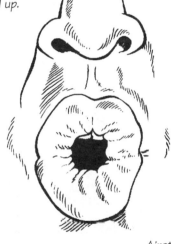

Tongue rests on
bottom of mouth.

Harmonica played
straight on,
not on side of lips.

Single note hole
shaped like a vertical oval.

Airstream ( as large as possible)
is channeled by the way you pucker.
Remember: control and focus.

No part of lip obstructs harmonica
hole or airstream.

# How to Avoid Running Out of Breath

Consider your draw notes: When you take a deep breath, you can gasp enough air to fill your lungs in about half a second. Or you can take a long, slow inhaled breath into an imaginary airbag in your stomach that lasts five, ten, twenty or thirty seconds. Deep level breathing means breathing this slow way. Try the following exercise to get in touch with the correct way to deep breathe.

## Doc's Special Pacing-the-Clock Exercise
## For Deep Breathing Perfection

Set yourself in front of a clock and play a long, soft note. Say, a 4 blow. See how long you can make that 4 blow last. Five seconds? Ten? Fifteen? Hint: As you run out of air, push from your diaphragm.   When you're almost out of breath *draw*. Gently pull the air into your belly, not your lungs.  Go back and forth between your blows and draws, making each last as long as possible. When you start, it may be only five ticks, but if you refine your technique, your breaths will last as long as thirty. Each improvement in time will mark an improvement in your harp-playing.

1.  Keep your shoulders down, not hunched up.

2.  When drawing, make sure you're not doing the ½ second gasp into your lungs—rather pull air slowly into that imaginary airbag.

3.  Do not stand erect with your chest out. Keep your body relaxed.

4.  Seek balance and comfort between your blows and draws. If you're out of breath, you're out of luck.

5.  Although it might seem dismal at first, learning to breathe correctly is one of the easiest of all harmonica techniques to master. Doc's Pacing-the-Clock Exercise is the key.

# Reversing Your Breath

Reversing your breath is going from draw to blow and blow to draw—something you do a lot of when you play the ol' harpoon. If you were to make these reversals from your lungs or diaphragm, your music would be seriously out of control and your audience (if there were anyone left to listen) would be picking you up off the floor after the first minute. The correct way to reverse your breath is **in your mouth**, breathing shallowly. For instance . . .

Imagine you're drinking a milkshake. When you draw, the shake travels a couple of inches up the tube. If you blow, it travels back down. Imagine making it go back and forth, an inch at a time. The reversal of breath happens in the front of your mouth. This is the same way the blow and draw happens when you play harp—in the front of your mouth, never your lungs! To get this into your mind, practice going back and forth between blow and draw on hole number 4. Control and focus that reversal of breath from a point just behind your teeth and let air leak into your lungs as you need it.

*reverse breath here*

*Slow breathe here*

## Silence Can Be Golden

When and if you do start to get winded (and we all do), calmly take the harp from your mouth, and take a breath, or let one out. Music naturally has lots of pauses in it. Take advantage of these pauses to breathe. Let the beat of your music take over. At such times, what you will be playing is *silence*. And silence is part of music, too.

# Playing the Songs

Now let's take a look at how you can use blows, draws, chords, single notes and tonguing to play some of the great songs notated later in this book. The notation works this way: a circled number means draw, an uncircled number means to blow and the dot means to tongue the note you're already playing.

Give it a try on the first line of the American masterpiece, "America." To start, you may want to play a 4 blow and then try humming the song to help yourself get the right start. After this little preparation, put the harp in your mouth and start playing it.

4    •    ④   ③   4   ④

**My country 'tis of thee**

circled numbers mean draw
uncircled mean blow
dot means tongue

Let me walk you through it: Play a 4 blow and tongue the note to express the words *"My coun . . ."*

Now play the *". . . try"* with a 4 draw.

Next, draw and swivel the harp to hole 3 for the 3 draw, play 4 blow, and 4 draw.

Following the notation, do this again and again until you have it pat. Then go on to the next line and the next line after that. For more of Doc's splendid suggestions on putting it all together, keep reading.

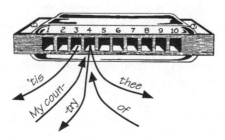

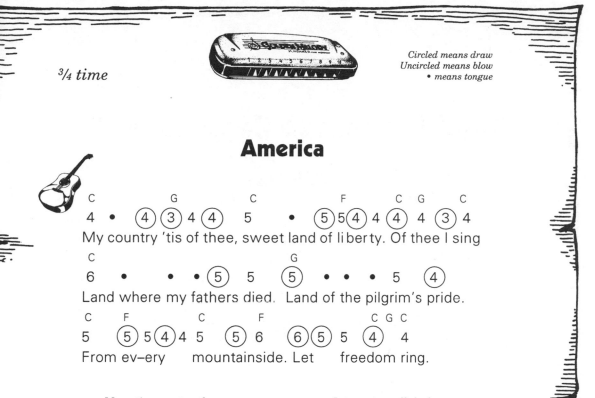

*Circled means draw*
*Uncircled means blow*
• *means tongue*

# America

| C | | G | | C | | F | C | G | C |
|---|---|---|---|---|---|---|---|---|---|

4 • ④ ③ 4 ④ 5 • ⑤ 5④ 4 ④ 4 ③ 4
My country 'tis of thee, sweet land of li ber ty. Of thee I sing

| C | | | | G | | | |
|---|---|---|---|---|---|---|---|

6 • • • ⑤ 5 ⑤ • • • 5 ④
Land where my fathers died. Land of the pilgrim's pride.

| C | F | | C | F | | C G C |
|---|---|---|---|---|---|---|

5 ⑤ 5④ 4 5 ⑤ 6 ⑥⑤ 5 ④ 4
From ev–ery mountainside. Let freedom ring.

My native country, thee,
Land of the noble free,
Thy name I love;
I love thy rocks and rills,
Thy woods and dimpled hills
My heart with rapture thrills
Like that above.

Let music swell the breeze,
and ring from freedom's trees
sweet freedom's song.
Let mortal tongues awake;
Let all that breathe partake
Let rocks their silence break
The sound prolong.

Our fathers' God to Thee
Author to Liberty
To thee we sing.
Long may our land be bright
With freedom's holy light,
Protect us by Thy might
Great God, our king.

These are Samuel Francis Smith's words to the old English hymn, "God Save the Queen." First sung in 1831, it became popular with the North during the Civil War and has become an unofficial national anthem. There are patriotic tunes with different lyrics, set to the same melody, in Switzerland and Germany. This song sounds equally good played in chords and single notes. Play it in chords by playing the notes with a mouth large enough to play three or four holes at one time. Then make adjustments for best sound. Incidentally, the C's, G's and F's above the harmonica notation are the guitar chords. Use them when you jam with a buddy.

# Should I Learn to Read Music First?

As Niccolo Paganini, the Italian violin virtuoso of the 18th and 19th centuries observed, you don't learn to read before you learn to talk, so why learn to read music before learning how to play it? So to answer the question posed above: No. Don't learn to read music in order to learn the harmonica. Later, however, once you've got your sound, reading could be useful—especially if you want to do session work or move into the chromatic harmonica.

There's another reason why beginning harmonica-playing and music-reading are a little like oil and water. The ten-hole diatonic harmonica is set up to play in only one key, and if you want to play in another key, you must pick up another key of harmonica. As a result, the notes change location with every different key of harmonica you pick up.

If learning to read music is important to you, yes, it can be done on a harmonica. But Doc's suggestion is to learn using a piano or keyboard. These instruments give you a good tone simply by the pressing of a key. As you are undoubtedly finding out, good tone from a harmonica is far more demanding. Plus, on these instruments, the notes don't change location when you change key.

Paganini notwithstanding, I realize that people who already read music may want a chart like the one below. So here it is: the location of each note on the musical staff—on the C harmonica only. Good luck—and please, don't slow down your music playing with music reading. For most of us, it will only be an obstacle.

Location of Notes on a C Harp

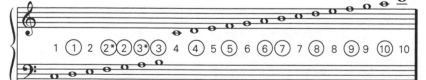

*Circled means draw*
*Uncircled means blow*
*\* means bend (explained later in book)*

# What about Tongue-Blocking?

Years ago, the most popular way to play a single note was to make your mouth big enough to play four holes at one time, and to block off three of the holes with your tongue. Then when you blew or drew, and if you had your tongue on the harp just right, you'd play that open hole. If you wanted to play a chord to accompany yourself, you could lift your tongue and a chord would ring out.

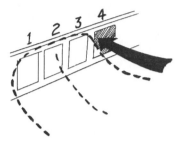

*Tongue covers holes 1, 2 and 3. Airstream enters hole 4*

The name of this technique is *tongue-blocking*. A lot of harmonica instruction still tells people to play this way. And, a lot of harmonica players still do. So why do I teach you to pucker? The problem with tongue-blocking is that it's *much* harder to get single notes this way, and once you're playing them, it's very difficult to bend them. Also, trying to tongue for precise phrasing and rhythm is awkward as heck.

I've got to take this one step further. If you already tongue-block and you feel stuck in a rut, I suggest you stop this antique technique for awhile so you can learn to pucker. Then, having the ability the tongue-block *and* pucker, you'll have some very powerful options. For instance . . .

## Octaves: An Advanced Tongue-Blocking Technique

Instead of placing your tongue on holes 123 and playing the open 4, try blocking holes 2 and 3 and letting the air go into holes 1 and 4. If you can get both these notes to come ringing through simultaneously, you'll get a sound like an accordion. I love it! This is called "playing octaves"—an advanced harp technique and not one beginners should get stuck on. The true message here is **learn to pucker for single notes,** then work with the many techniques of tongue-blocking.

# Moving the Harp from Hole to Hole

Well, you want your music to be smooth don't you? Moving the harmonica from one hole to the next is an essential part of harp playing. Doc's got a few rules to try on.

**Rule 1: Move the harmonica, not your head!!!!** You may need to watch yourself in the mirror to be sure you're doing this right.

**Rule 2:** Move the harmonica as though your lips were greased . If you jerk the harp around, your music will sound jerky. Instead make your moves **smooth and fluid.**

**Rule 3:** When moving just one hole on the harp, say from 3 to 4, **drag the harp on your lower lip,** making the lip itself serve as a guide in how far to move the harmonica. On the other hand, when moving more than one hole, slide the harp between your lightly moistened lips, just like a typewriter carriage.

**Rule 4:** Do not take the harmonica out of your mouth and put it back in as you search for notes. **Keep the harp in your mouth** and smoothly slide or drag it. Don't slam on the brakes. Rather, glide to a stop. No need to hurry, and always avoid choppiness or gaps of silence between the notes.

**Rule 5:** If you're playing, say, a 4 draw, and want to move to 5 blow, *do not* **stop the 4 draw in order to change the air direction** and move the harp. Instead, simply start to blow as you're still drawing and slide the harp to 5 at exactly that moment. Nine times out of ten, even beginners will get it right when they do it this way.

**Rule 6:** If you're playing a 4 draw and need to move to a 5 draw, there's no need to tongue or stop your breath. **Simply continue drawing and slide the harp** until it locks onto the new note. It'll sound great.

**Rule 7: Always practice slowly,** and then speed up.

# The Best Way to Learn Songs

Playing the melodies that follow, you'll be sliding from hole to hole, and going from blow to draw (or vice versa), and tonguing, all pretty much at the same time. There's a lot to do, and, if you make the mistake of over-thinking while playing, a flub-up is imminent. (This, from years of experience flubbing-up.)

Clearly, the best way to learn songs is to **isolate the first two notes and play them over and over.** After playing these two notes successfully a few times, add the third note and repeat the first three notes again and again, then add the fourth note, the fifth, the six note and so on until you have the entire line and eventually the entire song.

Each time you add a note, your goal is a smooth sound with no hesitation, gaps of silence or choppiness. **Your eventual overall goal should be to play the whole song without reading the notation, and without having to think.** (Blessed relief!) At this point, the song is inside you, ready to come out. All you have to do it *feel* it.

Also, be sure to put the notation aside. Remember what the first note is and play it. Add the second note and play that. Then add the third, fourth and fifth notes, and so on. It's easy to learn a song by heart when you add one note at a time. Try this and I know you'll be amazed when you start playing things you never thought you could in a real short period of time.

*Although it seems most harmonica players are of the male persuasion, many women (and children) have learned to play, and Doc hopes many, many more. If you're a woman or a child, pick up that harmonica and do it!*

# Doc Gindick's "Problem Hole" Miracle Meditation Exercise

You're tooting along, having a good time, and suddenly you hit a hole that just won't make a sound. Or else the sound that it does make is enough to make you want to say "Excuse me," and leave the room in shame. Most likely, this note is 2 draw or 3 draw, but it can also be one of the high notes 7, 8, 9 and 10 draw and blow.

The problem is every hole and every reed has a different requirement for producing a sound. Your job is to teach yourself what those requirements are and to make adjustments as you play the harp. This is where Doc's Miracle Meditation Exercise comes in. When you discover a hole you can barely play, stop everything, and take the time to focus on that hole, make your best single note pucker there, **and blow and draw, blow and draw, over and over, allowing yourself to breathe *only* through that hole.**

Do not take the harmonica from your mouth. In fact, pretend that the only way you can breathe is through that little hole. Then try in different ways to get an open, clear unimpeded airstream through the hole.

The one thing that seems to help most often with the lower draw notes is to draw a bit of air through your nostrils. The feeling is that you're pulling the note up to the top of your head. Also: Cut the volume of air by a third, by half, by seventy-five or even ninety per cent. Instead of forcing the note, coax it, become its friend, and eventually its master.

When the note finally rings through, it should be rich, resonant and full. What a feeling! There might even be a slight echo coming from the harp. Doing this exercise in a calm, meditative state of mind guarantees success.

# Combining Chords, Harmonies and Single Notes

Although the songs in this book are notated for single notes, it's possible to play many of them in chords—getting more than one note at a time.  For instance, the song "America" sounds excellent when you play it two to three notes at a time instead of single notes.

The following notation is just one way to do this.  Use mine or feel out your own.

34 • (34) (23) 34 (34)
My country 'tis of thee
45 • (45) 34 (23) 23
Sweet land of lib – er – ty
(34) 34 (1234) 1234
Of thee I sing

Here's a suggestion: first time through, play it in chords.  Second time, single notes.  Third time, chords and single notes.  It would also be possible to tongue-block octaves 1 and 4 blow on the opening and closing words of the song. This arrangement I leave to you.

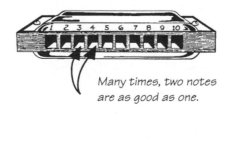

*Many times, two notes are as good as one.*

# Hand Talk on the Harp

Finger grip—works well with smaller hands. It's only necessary to form cup behind holes 1-4

*"Check out that harp player, hands cupped to his mouth, fingers dancing, opening, closing, fluttering like musical bird wings. Sounds coming outta the harp are pulsing, getting fat and thin, talking, yeah, saying words just beyond the range of human language, moving in and out of my eardrums like a sonic wave. How in the heck is he doing that?"*

By cupping your hands to create an airtight, air pocket **behind the lower notes** of your harmonica, you can mellow the tone of your instrument. By opening your hands as you play a note, you can make the harp say "wah." By fluttering one hand against the other, you can get a beautiful vibrato that sounds like "wah wah wah wah wah."

It's important to relax the flesh in your palms, the flesh between your fingers and the entire hand in general. (If your hands hurt, they're too tight). When you move your hands to a closed or open position, be sure not to move them too fast, or your sounds will be ragged and jerky. Make those movements fluid and smooth, like dancers.

*Palm grip—works well with large hands. Note position of right thumb*

Also, no matter how you choose to form your cup, here are three of Doc's favorite tips:

- Using the finger grip, cup the harp towards the back of the instrument so your fingers don't keep your lips from their rightful puckered placement well over the plates of the harp.

- Using either grip, try to anchor your hands so that opening and closing your cup doesn't jar the harmonica from its single note position.

- Move only the part of your hand that opens and closes the cup. You may need to watch yourself in the mirror as you practice this.

Use the illustrations here as starting places as you find the way of cupping, opening and closing your hands that works best for you. Good notes to start on are 3 blow and 4 blow. Close your hands. Then gently open them. Try to get your harp to say *wa*. Then get it to say *wa wa wa*.

If you're not having any success, examine your cupped hands for hidden openings that might be allowing the air to escape. Rearrange your fingers so that cup is airtight. Remember, you only need to cup the lower holes of the harp. Be patient and calm as you teach your baby to talk.

# Ready to Play?

The next few pages present the songs of **Harmonica Americana.** You can play them on any key of 10-hole diatonic harmonica. Feel free to flip through the pages and find that tune with which you have a special connection. Don't expect to learn the songs immediately. Rather, use the exercises, ideas and techniques presented earlier in this book as you practice daily. The idea is to let your inborn musical talent unfold over a period of time. The more you play—patiently, lovingly and in a spirit of fun and appreciation— the better you will get.

## About The Guitar Notation . . .

No two instruments go as well together as the harp and guitar. As a matter of fact, like Doc Watson, Bob Dylan, Donovan, Bruce Springsteen, Woody Guthrie, Ramblin' Jack Elliot, Jesse "Lonecat" Fuller and Neil Young, I like to play harp and guitar at the same time. I call it playing the *guitarmonica*. That's probably why I've placed simplified guitar chord notation above the harmonica hole numbers. Now, these chords are strictly for those who bang around a bit on the ol' axe. If you're working with the harmonica only, ignore these C's, F's, G's and A minors. On the other hand, if there's a guitarist in the house—instant jam session!

## The Arrangements

How's that ol' Sinatra song go? *I did it myyyyy way!* What Doc's trying to impart here is I play my music the way that works best for me and I teach you what I know. I love simple, primitive, heartfelt music and I guess my arrangements lean pretty far in that direction. Also, I wanted to make the arrangements as easy as possible, and this sometimes meant leaving out notes or complex guitar chords. So you may want to look at my arrangements as starting places for arrangements of your own. That's what traditional music means.

## The Songs and Their Histories

Learning to play songs like "Shenandoah" and "Red River Valley" is like dipping your hands into a treasure chest of gold. No doubt about it . . . these are *great* songs (just check out the lyrics!)—incredibly rich in texture and meaning, an essential part of our American culture. Knowing something of their histories revitalizes these tunes in our minds, so along with reprinting many lyrics I've also told little stories about how the songs intertwine with our country's past. These are stories you can pass on when you get around to performing for friends.

## Using the Notation and the Lyrics

Circle means draw. Uncircled means blow. Dot means tongue the note you're already playing. Here are some last minute tips: Play smoothly! Give the tune a beat by tapping your foot. Don't forget to make your tonguing crisp and in most cases to try to match the cadence of the lyrics. Play in single notes *and* chords. Keep a soft mouth, a soft hand. Be musical. If you feel stuck, try mentally singing (or humming) what you're trying to play. This will help you transfer the musical and rhythmic feeling of your imagination into your harmonica-playing. If you want to play your harmonica with feeling, sing with feeling. In the long run, feeling's what it's all about.

## The Tape Cassettes

Two tape cassettes teaching you the techniques and songs of **Harmonica Americana** are available. In fact, I made 'em just for you. If you don't have 'em, get 'em at the address listed in the back of the book. Incidentally, all the music on the tapes are for your C harp. And now, let's play some music!

# One-Minute Guitar Lesson

I admit it. I love the axe, the gitfiddle, the strung box, the six-string wonder. Here's what Doc can tell you about guitar-playing in a hundred words or less:

1. **Get a guitar.** Find the local **authentic** acoustic guitar place or catalog house and talk to them. There's usually no need to spend more than $150. Possibly less. Important? Good tone, good action. Used guitars are fine (some say better) and Japanese makes are O.K.

2. **Tune those strings.** Suggestion: Get an electronic guitar tuner. Pluck a string and it tells you whether you're sharp, flat or right on. Solves a big problem for less than two sawbucks.

3. **Get yourself a chord book** and learn the easier chords of C, F, G, A minor and E minor. Learn to strum or fingerpick and to hit that bass string as you work with the songs in this book. (Unless you want to be Andrés Segovia, fire any guitar teacher who forces you start off with scales!)

4. **Accept pain.** Pressing those strings will make your fingers hurt—until you get callouses. Live with it, bubby. The pain will go away as your fingers get tough. And they will. Just stay with it.

5. **No, your fingers are not too big or small.** (Everyone thinks that at first.) Be agressive in your fingering. Stretch out. Move your thumb on the back of the guitar's neck. Keep working on it!

6. **Get a guitar teacher.** If he or she is good, it's worth every penny. But first, the harmonica!

*Want to play harp and guitar at the same time? Get yourself a "rack" at your local music store (or from the resources listed in the back of this book), tune up, and start strumming. Once you've gotten the guitar going, try blowing and drawing that harp. It's tough at first, but soon becomes second nature.*

# Chapter Five

# THE SONGS OF HARMONICA AMERICANA

*The following songs are under public domain,
which means you can play, perform, teach and
record them without having to pay royalties.
Yahooo!*

*They're also some of the greatest,
most enduring tunes ever composed.*

*Because of the popularity of these songs, many
slight variations have appeared over the years.
Therefore, the following notations may differ
from the way you learned these tunes
on your granddaddy's knee.*

*Make adjustments and have fun with them.*

## The Mental Run-Through

*Before* you actually pick up your harp to learn a song, *read* the song and mentally hum the notes to yourself, pretending to be blowing, drawing, tonguing and sliding the harp from hole to hole. This mental run-through will help a lot once you've got harp in mouth.

# Down in the Valley — Traditional

C                                             G
3     4 (4) 5 4 5 • (4) 4 (4)
Down in the valley, the valley so low.

C                                              C
3 (3) (4) (5)(4)(3) 4 (4) 4
Hang your head ov–er, hear the wind blow.

C                                            G
3     4 (4) 5    4    5    6 • (4)
Hear the wind blow, dear, hear the wind blow.

C                                            C
3 (3) (4) (5)(4)(3) 4 (4) 4
Hang your head ov–er, hear the wind blow.

Roses love sunshine, violets love dew,
Angels in heaven know I love you.

If you don't love me, love whom you please.
Throw your arms round me, give my heart ease.

Build me a castle, 40 feet high,
So I can see him, as he rides by.

Write me a letter, send it by mail,
Send it in care of Birmingham jail.

Writing this letter containing three lines,
Answer my question, will you be mine?

About the time of the Louisianna Purchase in 1803, this folk song is said to have been sung by Appalachian pioneers, most of whom were English, Scottish and Irish. Old journals tell us it was later sung by followers of Daniel Boone as they made their hazardous journey westward over the highlands of Tennessee and Kentucky and into the Ozarks of Arkansas and Missouri. I love the timeless feeling of the lyrics and the way the ¾ time makes me want to sway back and forth.

## Can't Find the First Note of the Song?

Use your fingers to cover every hole but the one you're trying to play. Play that hole, get the sound in your mind, and then take your fingers away. Do this over and over until you can find the note without using your fingers. As you play and practice, the problem of finding notes on the harmonica will disappear, I promise.

*Circled means draw*
*Uncircled means blow*
*• means tongue*

# The Ol' Grey Mare – Traditional

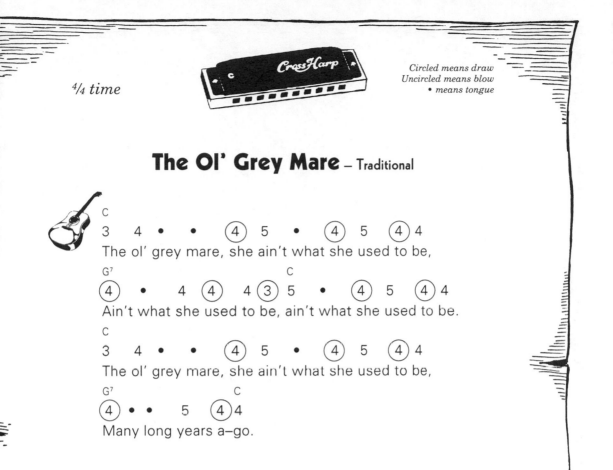

C
3  4  •  •  ④  5  •  ④  5  ④4
The ol' grey mare, she ain't what she used to be,

G⁷                          C
④  •  4  ④  4③5  •  ④  5  ④4
Ain't what she used to be, ain't what she used to be.

C
3  4  •  •  ④  5  •  ④  5  ④4
The ol' grey mare, she ain't what she used to be,

G⁷              C
④  • •  5  ④4
Many long years a–go.

The old grey mare she kicked on the whiffle tree,
Kicked on the whiffletree, kicked on the whiffle tree.
The old grey mare she kicked on the whiffle tree,
Many long years ago.

This matter-of-fact song is based on the African-American spiritual, "The Old Grey Mare Came Tearing Out of the Wilderness." (Which is how some people describe my harp-playing!) The move from 3 blow to 4 blow that opens the song needs to happen in one motion . . . single note 3 blow . . . continue blowing as you slide to 4 . . . tongue twice to create three syllables . . . then draw 4, blow 5 and so on. In addition, the song has an attractive swing feeling to it, almost jazzy. Try to put this jazzy feeling into your approach.

## Get Some Resonance in Your Tone

Keep working on your single note skills, making your mouth soft, your lips big, loose and puckered. Set the harmonica deep between those puckered lips, and push gently from your diaphragm to get a rich, full tone that resonates.

3/4 *time*

*Circled means draw*
*Uncircled means blow*
*• means tongue*

# Amazing Grace – John Newton

C                    F          C
3   4   5   •   ④   4   •   3

Amazing grace, how sweet the sound,

C              Am            G   G⁷
3    4    5   •    ④   6

That saved a wretch like me.

    C                    F          C
6  ⑥   •   5   ④   4   •   3

I once was lost, but now am found,

C              G      C
3    4    5   •   ④ 4

Was blind, but now I  see.

| | |
|---|---|
| Twas Grace that taught my heart to fear, | Through many dangers, toils and snares |
| And grace my fears relieved. | I have already come. |
| How precious did that grace appear | Tis grace that brought me safe thus far |
| The hour I first believed. | And grace will lead me home. |
| | |
| The Lord has promised good to me, | When we've been here 10,000 years, |
| His word my hope secures. | Bright shining as the sun, |
| He will my shield and portion be | We've no less days to sing God's praise |
| As long as life endures. | Than when we first begun. |

John Newton (1725-1807) was captain of an America-bound slave ship, when he experienced a spiritual conversion, turned his ship around, returned to Africa, and let the slaves go free. Like "Ol' Grey Mare," "Amazing Grace" starts off with a blow slide, only in this case, a slow one. Play 3 blow for the word "A," continue your blow and slide the harmonica to 4 for the syllable "maz," continue blowing and slide to 5 which you tongue to enunciate syllables "zing grace", and so on.

## Invent Your Own Techniques

As you fool around on the harmonica you'll discover some sounds and techniques that are all yours. Don't throw them away! The songs and sounds you make up yourself are part of your own style and are just as important as the songs and sounds I'm teaching you. Respect your own creative impulses. They're valuable.

Circled means draw
Uncircled means blow
• means tongue

# Oh! Susanna – Stephen Foster

C ⓸ 5    6  • ⑥ 6 5  4  ⓸  5 •  ⑧ 4  ④ G

Well, I come from A-la-bama with my banjo on my knee,

4  ④ 5    6  •   ⑥ 6 5  4 ④ 5    •   ④ •  4 G   C

And I'm going to Lou'–si–a–na, oh my true love for to see.

4  5    6  •  ⑥  6 5 4 ④  5   • ④ 4  ④ C                                    G

It rained so hard the day I left, the weather it was dry,

4  5 6  • ⑥ 6  5  4    ④ 5 •  ④   •   4 C                        G         C

The sun so hot I froze to death, Su-san-na, don't you cry.

⑤ • ⑥ •  •  6  •  5 4 ⓸ F            C                G

Oh Susanna! Oh, don't you cry for me,

4 ④ 5    6  • ⑥ 6 5 4 ④ 5    •  ④ • 4 C                                 G   C

For I come from A-la-ba-ma,    My true love for to see.

I had a dream the other night when everything was still,
I thought I saw Susannah dear a-coming down the hill.
The buckwheat cake was in her mouth, the tear was in her eye,
Says I, "I'm coming from the south, Susanna, don't you cry."

Next time you see a scruffy panhandler on some sidewalk playing harp for spare change, think of Stephen Foster and "Oh! Susanna." Stephen Collins Foster was born in Lawrenceville, Penn. on the 4th of July, 1826, to a prominent family that didn't know what to do about his dreamy and creative qualities. At age 20, he became a bookkeeper but his song "Oh! Susannah" was pirated by a minstrel singer, published without his knowledge, and became the anthem of the California gold miners. As a way to start his song-writing career Stephen "gave" the song to the W.C. Peters Publishing Company. Although it made him famous, he never received a penny for what is surely the most beloved song of our times.

## Kick that Critic Out of Town!

He's that feller that sits on your head and tells you what's wrong with your harp playing. It might not be perfect yet, but with time (and Doc's help) your music will improve. So here's my advice: Don't be a perfectionist. Instead, be a learner. Say affirmative things like "That sounds pretty good," and "Now I'm making music."

Circled means draw
Uncircled means blow
• means tongue

# On Top of Old Smokey – Traditional

C               F                            C

4 • 5 6 7 ⑥ • ⑤ 6 ⑥ 6

On top of Old Smokey, all covered with snow,

                   G                 C C⁷

4 • 5 6 • ④ 5⑤ 5 ④ 4

I lost my true lov–er, a courtin' too slow.

C⁷                  F                       C

4 • 5 6 7 ⑥ • ⑤ 6 ⑥ 6

Now courtin' is pleasure, and partin' is grief

C                      G                   C

4 •• 5 6 • ④ 5 ⑤ 5 ④ 4

And a false-hearted lov–er is worse than a thief.

A thief will just rob you and take what you have,
But a false-hearted lover will lead you to your grave.
And the grave will decay you and turn you to dust.
Not one boy in a hundred, a poor girl can trust.

They'll hug you and kiss you, and tell you more lies,
Than the cross ties on a railroad, or stars in the sky.
So come all you maidens and listen to me:
Never place your affection on a green willow tree.

For the leaves they will wither and the roots they will die,
You'll all be forsaken and never know why.
On Top of Old Smokey all covered with snow,
I lost my true lover a courtin' too slow.

This nugget is from the treasure trove of Appalachian musical contribution to our culture. It was an early 1800's mountain song that referred to a hazy peak in the Blue Ridge chain, a few miles from Ashville, North Carolina. During the westward migration of the 1840's and 50's, this song was sung in wagon trains, around campfires, in forts, parlors, and has become a part of our national heritage. Oh, could you pass the spaghetti? LEARN THIS SONG.  EVERYONE LOVES IT!

## Make That Harp Cry Like a Baby

This works best on the draw notes, say, 4 draw. Get a good single note. Make it start soft, get louder, then soft. Start with your hands closed and slowly open them. Add vibrato. Now put sadness into your sound, the same way you would into your voice. *Feel* it. That's right, make that harp cry like a little baby.

Circled means draw
Uncircled means blow
• means tongue

*3/4 time*

# Red River Valley – Traditional

C
3    4    5   •   •   •   ④   5   ④ 4
From this valley they say you are going,

C                                              G  G⁷
3   4   5   4   5   6   ⑤   5   ④
We will miss your bright eyes and sweet smile.

          C                              F
6  ⑤  5  •  ④  4  ④  5  6  ⑤
For they say you are taking the sunshine

               G                      C
3   •   •   ③   4   ④   5   ④ 4
That has brightened our pathways awhile.

Come and sit by my side if you love me,
Do not hasten to bid me adieu.
But remember the Red River Valley
And the one who has loved you so true.

As you go to your home by the ocean,
May you never forget those sweet hours
That we spent in the Red River Valley
And the love we exchanged 'mid the flowers.

Won't you think of the valley you're leaving,
Oh how lonely, how sad it will be?
Oh think of the fond heart you're breaking,
And the grief you are causing to me.

One of the greatest harmonica melodies of all, "Red River" is based on a popular song, "In the Bright Mohawk Valley," written by James Kerrigan in 1896. The melody lasted, but the words changed again and again—these reflecting the common sentiments of women left behind by wandering cowpokes. There are now hundreds of versions, including the Willie Nelson masterpiece on his album, "Red-Headed Stranger."

## Want Some Vibrato?

Some people have a beautiful throbbing tone that seems to vibrate its way right into your heart and soul. What is it? Vibrato. To add vibrato to your harmonica tone, make your deep stomach muscles vibrate just right as you blow and draw full-puckered single notes. This stomach vibration is similar to the "machine gun" sound kids make when playing cops and robbers. It's also close to the way people's voices vibrate when they try to imitate the speech of that wise old gent sitting on the front porch of the country store, *"I'm a-hundred-and-five and I still play harp!"* The main difference is that you do it with your breath, not your voice. Give it a try and you'll be amazed at how much emotion it adds to your harp's tone.

*⁴/₄ time*

# Old Folks at Home — Stephen Foster

```
    C                      F
5  ④   4 5 ④  4  7 ⑥ 7
```
Way down upon the Swanee River,

```
    C       G
6  5  4 ④
```
Far, far away.

```
    C                        F
5   ④   4 5 ④ 4 7 ⑥ 7
```
That's where my heart is turning e-ver,

```
    C                  G        C
6   5    4  ④  •   4
```
That's where the old folks stay.

All up and down the whole creation, Sadly I roam.
Still longing for the old plantation, and for the old folks at home.

All the world is sad and dreary, everywhere I roam,
Oh, brothers, how my heart grows weary, far from the old folks at home.

All around the little farm I wandered, when I was young.
Then many happy days I squandered, many the songs I sung.

When I was playing with my brother, happy was I.
Oh, take me to my kind old mother, there let me live and die.

One little hut among the bushes, one that I love,
Still sadly to my memory rushes, no matter where I rove.

When will I see the bees a-hummin', all around the comb?
When will I hear the banjo strummin' down in my good old home?

Stephen married Jane McDowell in 1850 and, during the first few years of his married life, he composed many of his finest songs, including "Old Folks at Home." The story goes he was stuck for the name of a river. The two he came up with were the "Pedee" and the "Yazoo." Finally, he and his brother Morrison looked through an atlas and discovered the "Suannie," a river that starts in Georgia and runs through Florida to the Gulf of Mexico. Suannie or "Swanee" seemed perfect and with the writing of this song, Stephen immortalized a river he had never seen. Published by the Firth & Pond Company of New York, this is a song that earned Stephen and his wife a few thousand dollars.

## Out of Breath?

Check out the section on breathing (pages 66-67). Remember to reverse your breath in the front of your mouth. Also, the softer you play, the easier to control the air. If your harmonica-playing sounds like hard work, neither you or your listener is going to enjoy it very much. Use Doc's "Pacing-the-Clock Exercise" to help make your harp-playing as effortless as talking. The main rule: no huffin' and puffin'! Take it easy.

*³/₄ time*

Circled means draw
Uncircled means blow
• means tongue

# Streets of Laredo — Traditional
## (the Cowboy's Lament)

C          G         C        G

3   4 •    (4) • •   5    (4) 4 (3) 3

As I walked out on the streets of La–re–do,

C        G        C     G

3   4 •    (4) • • 5 (4) 4 (4)

As I walked out in La–re–do one day,

C         G             C          G

6 • (5) 5 (5) 5 (4)    5 (4) 4    (3) 3

I spied a young cowboy wrapped up in white linen,

C            G      C   G C

3      4 (4) 5   (4) 5 (5) 5   4 (4) 4

Wrapped up in white lin–en as cold as the clay.

"I see by your outfit that you are a cowboy,"
These words he did say as I proudly stepped by,
"Come sit down beside me and hear my sad story.
I am shot in the breast and I know I must die."

"It was once in the saddle I used to go dashing,
It was once in the saddle I used to go gay,
First to the dramhouse and then to the card house,
Got shot in the breast and I know I must die."

"Let 16 gamblers come handle my coffin,
Let 16 cowboys come sing me a song,
Take me to the green valley and say a prayer over me,
For I'm a young cowboy and I know I've done wrong."

"O bang the drum slowly and play the fife lowly,
Play the dead march as you carry me on,
Take me to the graveyard and throw the sod over me,
For I'm a young cowboy and I know I've done wrong."

Although most of us probably remember this song as Marty Robbin's great hit, it's actually based on an 18th century British broadside, "The Unfortunate Rake." I love the way the melody goes at the line "I spied a young cowboy wrapped up in white linen." As you work on this line, and throughout the entire tune, strive for slow fluidity and smoothness.

89

## Let The Harmonica Play You

When you're fooling around on the harp, one note or sound frequently suggests the next. That's why it's important to kick back and let the sound of the harmonica do the work. Remember folks, it's an attitude. Instead of trying to figure the harp out, simply make a sound, and let that sound lead to another sound . . . and another. Think of harmonica playing as being in a good conversation. You may not know what you're going to say (or play) next, so you just sort of let it happen as it goes and trust where it wants to go . . . like ridin' a river.

*Circled means draw*
*Uncircled means blow*
*• means tongue*

# Frankie & Johnnie — Traditional

C
4 ④ 5 ⑥ 6 ⑥ 4 •
Frankie and Johnnie were lovers,

C
4 ④ 5 ⑥ 6 ⑥ 4
Oh Lordie how they could love.

F
7 • ⑥ 6 7 • • ⑥ 6
They swore to be true to each other,

F                    C
7 • • ⑦ ⑥ 6
true as the stars above.

C            G                          C
5 6 ⑥ ④ 6 • • ⑥ 6 5 4
He was her man, but he was doing her wrong.

Frankie and Johnnie went walking, John in his brand new suit,
"Then o' Lord," says Frankie, "don't my Johnnie Boy look cute. He . . .

Frankie went down to the corner just for a bucket of beer,
She said to the fat bartender, "Has my loving man been here? He . . .

"I don't want to cause you no trouble, and I don't want to tell you no lie,
but I saw your man an hour ago with a gal named Alice Bly,
And if he's your man, he's a doing you wrong."

Frankie looked over the transom and found to her great surprise,
that there on the bed sat Johnnie, a lovin' up Alice Bly. He. . .

Frankie drew back her kimono, she took out her little '44,
root a toot toot three times she snot, right through the hardwood floor.
She shot her man, cause he was doing her wrong.

The judge said to the jury, "It's as plain as plain can be,
This woman shot her lover, it's murder in the second degree.
He was her man, but he was doing her wrong.

Love, sex, adultery, murder . . . over 100 versions of America's
most popular blues ballad exist, and thousands of verses. (For
years it was known as "Frankie & Albert.") But who wrote it? And
when? Was it based on the St. Louis murder case of 1899? If so,
then why did people sing it on the Mississippi River in the 1840's?

## The Band in Your Mouth

And the players are: your lips which pucker and change shape, your tongue articulating the cadence of the words of the song, your throat opening and closing to control the airstream, the airstream itself, changing shape and direction quickly, easily, effortlessly— and they all play in the front of your mouth—powered by the deep slow breathing that comes from your gut.

O.K. boys, hit it!

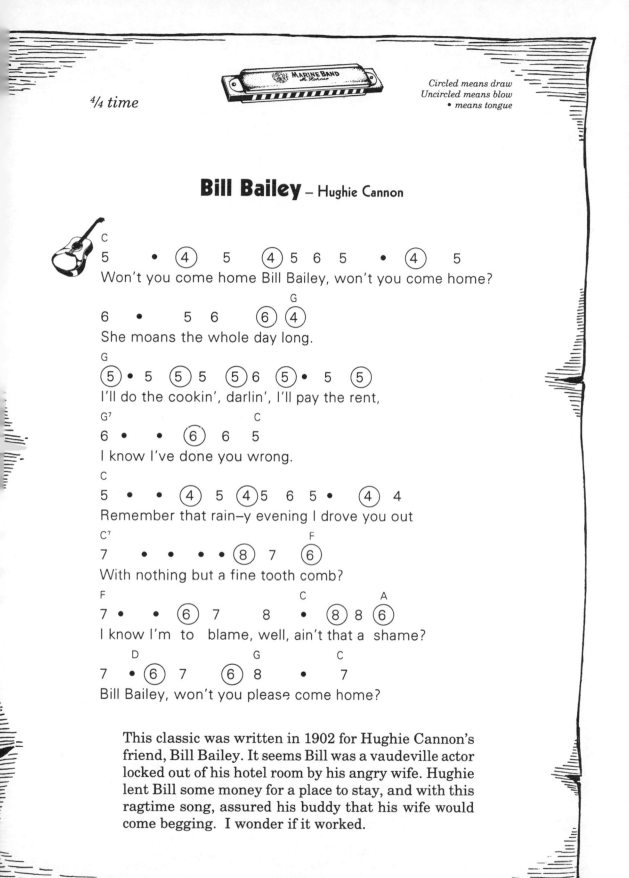

4/4 time

*Circled means draw*
*Uncircled means blow*
*• means tongue*

# Bill Bailey – Hughie Cannon

C
5 • ④ 5 ④ 5 6 5 • ④ 5
Won't you come home Bill Bailey, won't you come home?

                            G
6 • 5 6 ⑥ ④
She moans the whole day long.

G
⑤ • 5 ⑤ 5 ⑤ 6 ⑤ • 5 ⑤
I'll do the cookin', darlin', I'll pay the rent,

G⁷                       C
6 • • ⑥ 6 5
I know I've done you wrong.

C
5 • • ④ 5 ④ 5 6 5 • ④ 4
Remember that rain–y evening I drove you out

C⁷                         F
7 • • • • ⑧ 7 ⑥
With nothing but a fine tooth comb?

F                     C          A
7 • • ⑥ 7 8 • ⑧ 8 ⑥
I know I'm to blame, well, ain't that a shame?

        D              G          C
7 • ⑥ 7 ⑥ 8 • 7
Bill Bailey, won't you please come home?

This classic was written in 1902 for Hughie Cannon's friend, Bill Bailey. It seems Bill was a vaudeville actor locked out of his hotel room by his angry wife. Hughie lent Bill some money for a place to stay, and with this ragtime song, assured his buddy that his wife would come begging. I wonder if it worked.

## Soft, Loud, Soft

Add feeling to your songs by making the longer notes
start softly, get louder, and then gradually trail off.
This is also the best way to end songs.

Soft-loud-soft—it's the good Doc's formula for feeling.

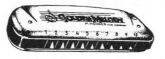

*3/4 time*

# Shenandoah – Traditional

```
       C                        F    C
   3   4  •  •  (4) 5  (5)(6)  6
   Oh Shenandoah, I long to see you.

       F              C
   7  (7)(6)  6  (6) 6  5  6
   A – way, you rolling river.

            Am                        C        Am
    5  6   (6)  •  •   5  6   5  (4)  4
    Oh   Shenandoah, I long to see you.

        C                   Am
    3   4   3      4   (6)  6
    A-way, we're bound a-way,

                F         G   C
    4    (4)  5     4  (4)  4
    Cross the wide Missou-ri.
```

Oh Shenandoah, I'm bound to leave you, away, you rolling river.
Oh Shenandoah, I'll not deceive you. Away, we're bound away, cross the wide Missouri.

Oh Shenandoah,  I've been a rover, away, you rolling river.
Oh Shenadoah, I'll be your lover. Away, we're bound away, cross the wide Missouri.

The trader loved an Indian maiden, away, you rolling river.
With furs and beads, his canoe was laden.  Away, we're bound away, cross the wide Missouri.

This hallmark harmonica song was an inland river chantey said to be sung by American and Canadian voyagers west of the Mississippi.  It takes its name from the Shenandoah Valley of Virginia, "land of big mountains" in the language of the Iroquois.  Its haunting melody evokes images of the Old West, and is the signature song of Charlie McCoy, myself and countless others harmonica players.

## Don't Stop Playing in the Middle of a Song

No matter how badly you feel you've botched up a song, don't stop playing it in the middle. Instead, try to recover and play that song to it's very end. The endings of songs are more important than the middles so give your tunes a soft-loud-soft grand finale.

*Circled means draw*
*Uncircled means blow*
*• means tongue*

# Beautiful Dreamer — Stephen Foster

C        F
7  ⑦ 7 6  5 ④  4 ④⑥
Beau–ti–ful dreamer, wake un–to me,

G         C
6 ⑦ ⑥ • 6 ⑤ • 5 ④ 5
Starlight and dewdrops are waiting for thee.

C        F
7  ⑦ 7 6 5 ④ 4 ④⑥
Sounds of the rude world heard in the day,

G         C
6 ⑦⑥ • 6 ⑤ • 5 ④4
Lulled by the moonlight have all passed away!

G     C
6 ⑤④③⑥ • 6 5 4
Beau–ti–ful dreamer, queen of my song,

D       G
7 ⑦ 7⑥ ⑧ 7 ⑦ 7 ⑥6
List while I woo thee with soft me–lo–dy.

C        F
7 ⑦ 7 6 5 ④ 4 ④⑥
Gone are the cares of life's bu–sy throng.

G         C
6 ⑦⑥• 6 ⑤ • 5 ④4
Beauti–ful dreamer awake un–to me!

This was one of Stephen's final compositions. To get money he had signed away most of the rights to his songs. He was drinking heavily and his health was failing. Jane left him and somehow he wrote the masterpiece above but couldn't get it published. Two years later, at age 37, he was found bleeding to death on the floor of his New York apartment. The song was published posthumously and to help sales, billed as the last he wrote. It's a sad story, but what an amazing song.

## Relax Your Body

Shoulders back, chest out, fists clenched, eyes wide open—many beginners feel they should almost stand at attention when they play harp. I think it's much better to have fun with your posture so long as it doesn't impede your breathing or keep you from expressing enthusiasm. So relax when you play harp, almost like an athlete—steady, calm and at ease.

*Circled means draw*
*Uncircled means blow*
*• means tongue*

# Camptown Races – Stephen Foster

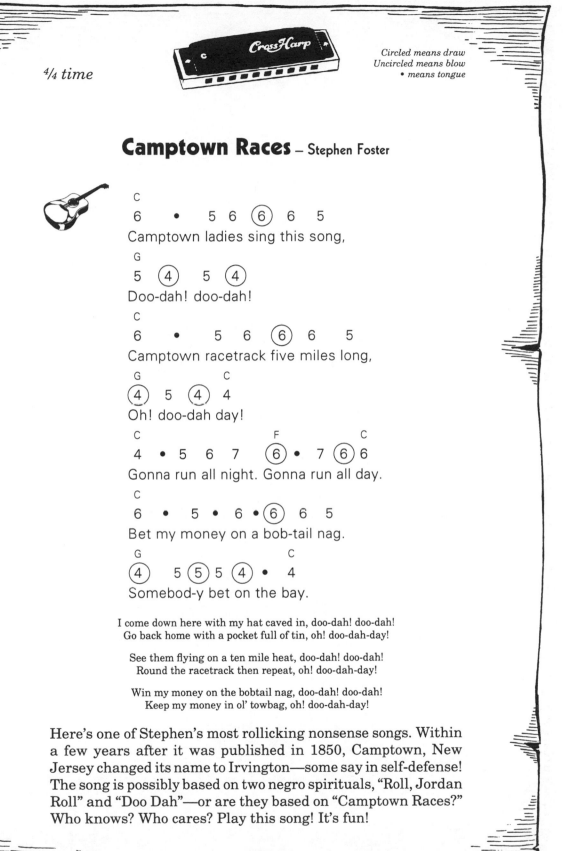

C
6  •  5  6  ⑥  6  5

Camptown ladies sing this song,

G
5  ④  5  ④

Doo-dah! doo-dah!

C
6  •  5  6  ⑥  6   5

Camptown racetrack five miles long,

G        C
④  5  ④  4

Oh! doo-dah day!

C                    F         C
4  •  5  6  7   ⑥  •  7  ⑥  6

Gonna run all night. Gonna run all day.

C
6  •  5  •  6  •⑥  6  5

Bet my money on a bob-tail nag.

G                      C
④   5  ⑤  5  ④  •   4

Somebod-y bet on the bay.

I come down here with my hat caved in, doo-dah! doo-dah!
Go back home with a pocket full of tin, oh! doo-dah-day!

See them flying on a ten mile heat, doo-dah! doo-dah!
Round the racetrack then repeat, oh! doo-dah-day!

Win my money on the bobtail nag, doo-dah! doo-dah!
Keep my money in ol' towbag, oh! doo-dah-day!

Here's one of Stephen's most rollicking nonsense songs. Within a few years after it was published in 1850, Camptown, New Jersey changed its name to Irvington—some say in self-defense! The song is possibly based on two negro spirituals, "Roll, Jordan Roll" and "Doo Dah"—or are they based on "Camptown Races?" Who knows? Who cares? Play this song! It's fun!

## Play With an Echo . . . echo . . . echo . . .

Because of the echo they provide, stairwells, showers, bathrooms are all great places to practice. Another good one is to pick up a phone, dial one number so you lose the dial tone and play into that. Works great till that recorded voice or siren telling you to hang up the phone comes on. One more idea: buy yourself a mike and an amplifier. Cup that mike in your hands and turn up the reverb. What a noise! Hearing yourself with an echo can really help you like your sound, and liking your sound can help you break through as a harp-player.

# Brahms' Lullaby — Johannes Brahms

```
            C                                    G
5 • 6 5   •   6    5 6 7 ⑦ ⑥ • 6
Lullaby and goodnight with  roses  be–side,
```

```
                                                    C
④ 5 ⑤ ④  •  5 ⑤    ④⑤⑦⑥ 6 ⑦  7
With  lil–lies all bedecked in    ba–by's  wee bed.
```

```
      F          C
4  •  7  ⑥ ⑤ 6
Lay thee down, now and rest.
```

```
      F          C
5  4 ⑤ 6 ⑥ 6
May thy slumber be blessed.
```

```
      F          C
4  •  7  ⑥ ⑤ 6
Lay thee down now and rest.
```

```
      F    G   C
5  4 ⑤  5 ④ 4
May thy slumber be blessed.
```

Lullaby and good night, thy mother's delight.
Bright angels beside my darling abide.
They will guard thee at rest, thou shalt wake on my breast.

Here's a great German song for you to play on a
great German instrument. The composer was born
in Hamburg, 1833, and wrote his "Lullaby" in the
mid 1860's, just about the time the harmonica was
gaining popularity in the U.S. It is a natural for the
harp, sounding beautiful played both in chords and
single notes. We'll never know whether Johannes
Brahms played the pocket piano, but if he didn't, he
should have.

## Play With Conviction

When learning a song, you may toot it out under your breath—sort of half-thinking, half-playing. This is understandable and O.K., but as soon as possible, be sure to close this book and start playing your harp with conviction. Close your eyes, flutter your hands with dramatic flourish, sway with the music, throw your whole self into it and refuse to worry about mistakes. If you do make a mistake, keep right on playing. Finish the song with a big soft-loud-soft grand finale—and work out the problems later.

4/4 time

Circled means draw
Uncircled means blow
• means tongue

# When Irish Eyes are Smiling

— Chauncey Alcott, George Graff, Jr. and Ernest Hall

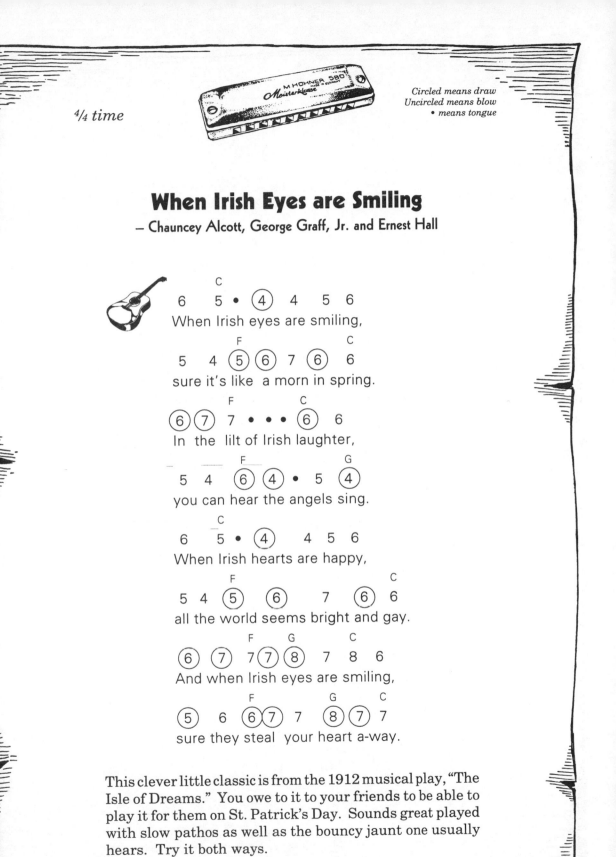

       C
6   5  •  ④  4  5 6
When Irish eyes are smiling,

       F         C
5  4 ⑤ ⑥ 7 ⑥  6
sure it's like  a morn in spring.

      F        C
⑥⑦ 7 • • • ⑥  6
In  the  lilt of Irish laughter,

        F        G
5  4  ⑥ ④ • 5 ④
you can hear the angels sing.

     C
6   5 • ④  4  5 6
When Irish hearts are happy,

      F          C
5 4 ⑤  ⑥   7  ⑥ 6
all the world seems bright and gay.

       F  G     C
⑥  ⑦  7⑦ ⑧  7  8 6
And when Irish eyes are smiling,

      F     G   C
⑤  6 ⑥⑦ 7  ⑧⑦ 7
sure they steal  your heart a-way.

This clever little classic is from the 1912 musical play, "The Isle of Dreams." You owe to it to your friends to be able to play it for them on St. Patrick's Day. Sounds great played with slow pathos as well as the bouncy jaunt one usually hears. Try it both ways.

## Keep Your Harmonica With You 24 Hours a Day

Make it a new habit—perhaps even a substitute for one you're trying to quit. Play in your car, your office, your favorite chair, when taking a walk (great way to get a slow, steady beat going). Play on your boat, in the garage, at the kitchen table, or in a hotel room. The main thing? Keep it with your 24 hours a day and consult with it often.

Circled means draw
Uncircled means blow
• means tongue

*⁴/₄ time*

# Stars and Stripes Forever – John Phillip Sousa
## (Be Kind to Your Web-Footed Friends)

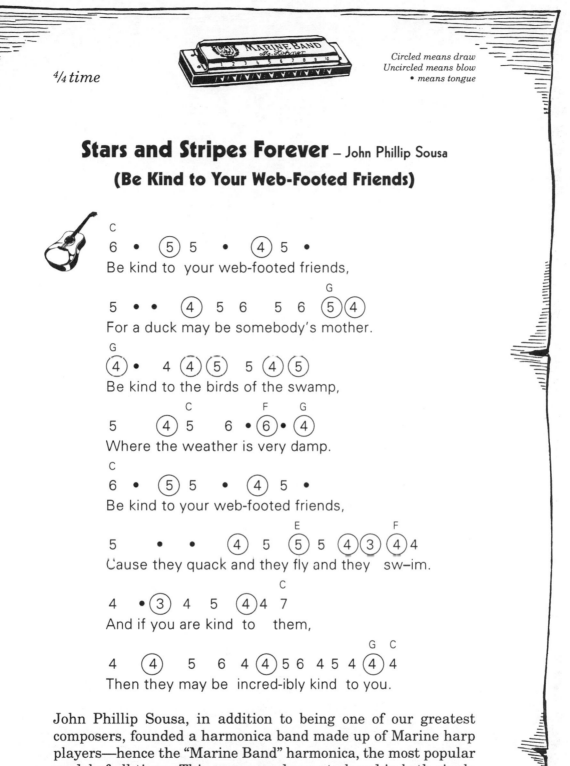

C
6 • ⑤ 5 • ④ 5 •
Be kind to  your web-footed friends,

                                           G
5 • • ④ 5 6   5 6 ⑤④
For a duck may be somebody's mother.

G
④ • 4 ④ ⑤ 5 ④ ⑤
Be kind to the birds of the swamp,

               C        F  G
5   ④ 5   6 • ⑥ • ④
Where the weather is very damp.

C
6 • ⑤ 5 • ④ 5 •
Be kind to your web-footed friends,

                      E            F
5 • • ④ 5 ⑤ 5 ④③④4
'Cause they quack and they fly and they   sw–im.

                           C
4 • ③ 4 5 ④4 7
And if you are kind  to   them,

                                     G C
4 ④ 5 6 4 ④ 5 6 4 5 4 ④ 4
Then they may be  incred-ibly kind  to you.

John Phillip Sousa, in addition to being one of our greatest composers, founded a harmonica band made up of Marine harp players—hence the "Marine Band" harmonica, the most popular model of all time.  This song sounds great played in both single notes and chords and is amazingly easy.  I apologize to ol' John Phillip for making you play it to these inane lyrics but I am unaware of any other words to this American classic.

## Slide It!!!!!

To make your motions smooth and fluid, keep a glass of water nearby for frequent mouth and lip-wetting. If you're just starting out, use your fingers to hold the harp on one end or the other. If you're cupping the harp for the *wa wa* effects, hold the harmonica with your hands, wrists, arms, elbows relaxed. As you go from hole to hole, remember to move the harmonica, not your head.

**⁴/₄ time**

*Circled means draw*
*Uncircled means blow*
*• means tongue*

# Battle Hymn of the Republic — Julia Ward Howe

C
6 • • • ⑤ 5 6 7 ⑧ 8 • • ⑧ 7
Mine eyes have seen the glory of the coming of the Lord,

    F
7 ⑦ ⑥ • • ⑦ 7 ⑦
He has trampled out the vintage

    C
7 ⑥ 6 ⑥ 6   5   6
where the grapes of wrath are stored.

C                Am
6 • • • • ⑤ 5   6
He has loosed the fateful lightening

    C           Am
7 ⑧ 8 • • ⑧   7
of his terrible swift sword.

    F     G       C
7 ⑧ • 7 ⑦ 7
His truth is marching on.

C                   F              C
6 ⑤ 5 6 7 ⑧ 8 7 ⑥ ⑦ 7 ⑦ 7 ⑥ 6 5
Glory, glory hal–le–lu–jah, Glo–ry, glory hal–le–lu–jah,

C   Am          C   Am      F      G      C
6 ⑤ 5 6 7 ⑧ 8 7   7 ⑧ • 7 ⑦ 7
Glory, glory hal–le–lu–jah, His truth is marching on.

Julia Howe, abolitionist/feminist, wrote these lyrics in 1861 while visiting Union troops in Washington, D.C. The melody is based on the earlier song "John Brown's Body." One way to play it is to imagine yourself on a Civil War hillside, opposing armies of blue and gray camped all around. Then start slowly, making every note count (as though trumpeted down directly from heaven) and let the whole thing build up to the most inspirational, emotional and spiritually rousing tone possible.

## Play a Fast Song Slowly

Many times the first step in learning to play a song is to play it very slowly. If possible, memorize it one note or phrase at a time, and learn to enjoy playing it as a ballad instead of a jig. As time goes on, you'll pick up speed naturally. And don't forget the power of tonguing!

*Circled means draw*
*Uncircled means blow*
*• means tongue*

# Turkey in the Straw — Traditional

C
8 ⑧ 7 • ⑧ 7 5 ⑤ 6 ⑥ 6 5 6
Well I had an old hen and she had a wooden leg.

                          G
7 ⑧ 8 • • 7 ⑧ 8 ⑧ •
Just the best old hen that ever laid an egg.

           C
8 ⑧ 7 • ⑧ 7 5 ⑤ 6 ⑥ 6 5 6
Well she laid more eggs than an–y hen on the farm,

                                G             C
7 ⑧ 8 9 • • • 8 7 ⑧ 8 7 ⑧⑦ 7
But an–other little drink would–n't do her an–y harm.

C
5 6 • • • 5 6 •
Turkey in the hay, hey, hey hey!

F
⑤⑥ • • • ⑤ ⑥ •
Turkey in the straw, straw, straw, straw!

C                                          G
⑥ ⑦ 7 • • 6 • • 5 • ④
Pick 'em up, shake 'em up, any way at all,

          C                          G            C
4 ④ 5 6 • • 5 4 ④ 5 4 ④③ 4
And hit up a tune called a'Turkey in the straw.

Originally played on fiddle and banjo, this is the classic
American rural tune. You can smell the furrowed fields,
and the animals in the stalls. Its cock-eyed humor has been
sung to horses, husbands, wives, children, dogs, and yes,
turkeys. Despite all this, it is not that easy a song to play,
and should be considered a real harmonica accomplishment
when you've got it down.  Feel free to play it *your* way.

## Count On Improvement

Whenever you start to feel discouraged, think of your harp-learning as being like baking a cake. If you play harp every day, using the instruction and songs for your recipe, thinking about what you're doing and earnestly trying to get better, that cake will cook. No matter who you are, or what your experience, improvement is *always* the natural consequence of the time you spend playing and the degree of mental concentration you pour into that time. (Incidentally, no matter how long you keep *this* cake in the oven, it will not burn!)

*³/₄ time*

Circled means draw
Uncircled means blow
• means tongue

# America the Beautiful

— Katherine Lee Bates and Samuel A. Ward

```
    C                   G              F      G        C   G
    6  •  5  •  6  •  ⑤  ④    5  ⑤ 6  ⑥    ⑦  6
    Oh beautiful, for spacious skies, for amber waves of grain,

       C                   G            D                G   G⁷
    6  •  5  •    6  •  ⑤④  ⑧ 7  ⑧ 8  ⑥⑧
    For purple mountain majesties  above thy fruited plain,

       C          G              F        G        C   C⁷
    6  8  ⑧ •  7  •  ⑦ •  7  ⑧  ⑦ ⑥   6  7
    Ame–ri–ca, Ame–ri–ca, God shed his grace on thee,

          F              C      Am
    7  •   ⑥  •  7  •  6  •
    And crown thy good with brotherhood

       F      G      C
    6  ⑥  7  6  ⑧  7
    From sea to shining sea.
```

Oh beautiful, for pilgrim feet whose stern impassioned stress,
A thoroughfare for freedom beat across the wilderness.
America! America! God mend thine every flaw,
Confirm thy soul in self control, thy liberty in law.

Oh beautiful, for heroes proved in liberating strife.
Who more than self their country loved, and mercy more than life.
America! America! May God thy gold refine.
Til all success be nobleness and every gain divine.

On a trip west to Pike's Peak in 1893, Katherine Bates, a vibrant and inspired English teacher at Wellesly College, was inspired by "spacious skies" and "purple mountain majesties," and wrote the poem, "America the Beautiful" which was published in the magazine, *The Congregationalist* in 1895. The poem created quite a stir and many composers tried to give it a melody. Finally, a contest was held, and out of 900 entries, the winner was "Materna," a hymn based on an old set of verses called "Oh Mother Dear Jerusalem," composed by Samuel Ward, a New Jersey musician and music dealer back in 1888. It is doubtful that the collaborators ever met—since Ward died in 1903.

## Play That Harp At Different Volumes

Play your harmonica softly as well as loudly. Also learn to make a note start softly, get louder, then trail off. This is one of the best ways to add feeling. When you do play more loudly, push from your diaphragm. (rather than blowing and drawing harder.) The concept of getting louder and softer in one song (or on one note) is called **dynamics** and is one of those easy little details that can make you sound like you've been playing your whole life.

*Circled means draw*
*Uncircled means blow*
*• means tongue*

# Old Rugged Cross – George Bennard

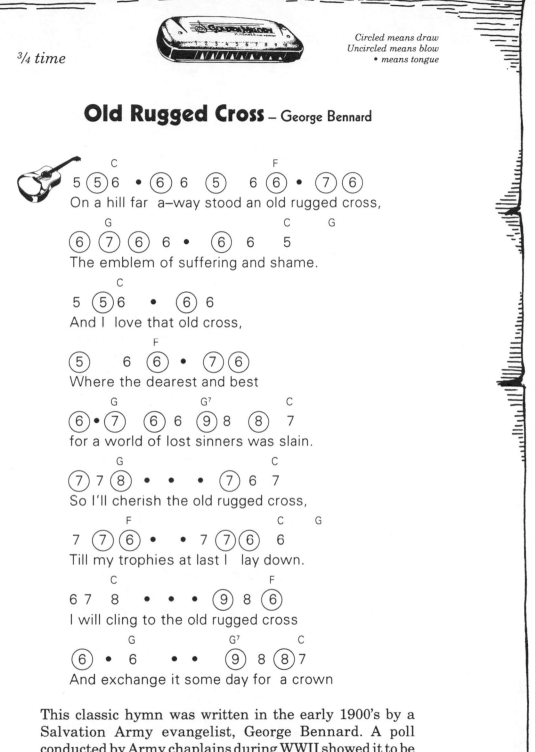

     C                         F
5 ⑤ 6 • ⑥ 6 ⑤ 6 ⑥ • ⑦ ⑥
On a hill far a–way stood an old rugged cross,

        G                    C   G
⑥ ⑦ ⑥ 6 • ⑥ 6 5
The emblem of suffering and shame.

       C
5 ⑤ 6 • ⑥ 6
And I love that old cross,

             F
⑤ 6 ⑥ • ⑦ ⑥
Where the dearest and best

       G          G⁷       C
⑥ • ⑦ ⑥ 6 ⑨ 8 ⑧ 7
for a world of lost sinners was slain.

       G               C
⑦ 7 ⑧ • • • ⑦ 6 7
So I'll cherish the old rugged cross,

       F               C   G
7 ⑦ ⑥ • • 7 ⑦ ⑥ 6
Till my trophies at last I lay down.

     C                  F
6 7 8 • • • ⑨ 8 ⑥
I will cling to the old rugged cross

       G            G⁷   C
⑥ • 6 • • ⑨ 8 ⑧ 7
And exchange it some day for a crown

This classic hymn was written in the early 1900's by a
Salvation Army evangelist, George Bennard. A poll
conducted by Army chaplains during WWII showed it to be
not only the all-time favorite gospel song, but also the most
popular of all Protestant hymns. I, for one, think it has a
beautiful, passionate melody and is great for the harmonica.

## Playing Those High Notes

The high notes are among the hardest on your harp. When you set about learning to play them, use Doc's Pure Herbal Tonic "Problem Hole" Miracle Meditation Exercise. Camp out on 8 blow and draw and stay there, playing this rascal over and over, making small adjustments until a good tone comes through. Do this a little bit every day, and remember to be patient and receptive.

Adjusting the tiniest things—the position of your tongue, the angle of the harp, the amount of tension or relaxation in your pucker, the amount of air coming through your nose, the fineness of your airstream, the set of your jaw, the curve of the flesh between your nostril and your upper lip—can make a huge difference in your success or failure to make the high notes play. One thing is for sure: ol' harp is *not* going to do it your way. You're going to have to do it ol' harp's way. As you blow and draw these high notes over and over, listen for instructions from the reed itself.

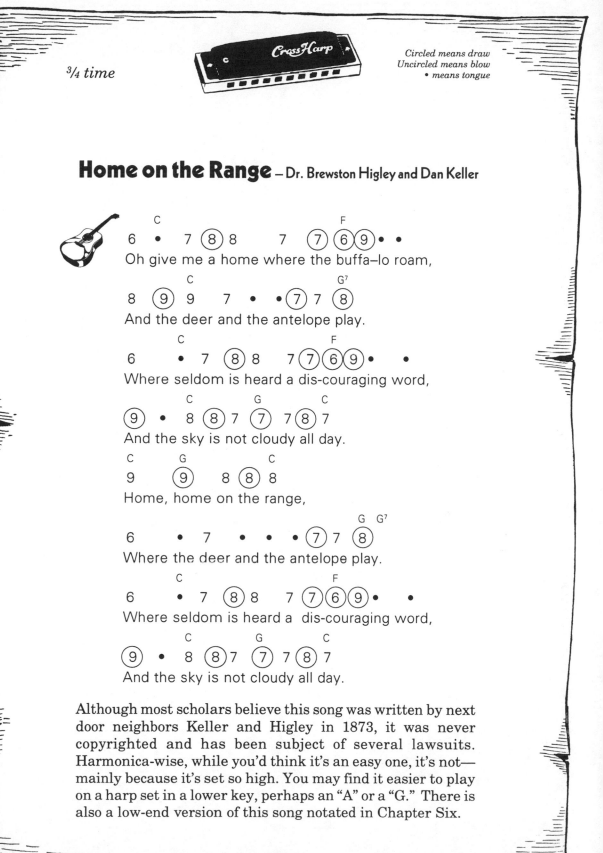

*Circled means draw*
*Uncircled means blow*
*• means tongue*

# Home on the Range — Dr. Brewston Higley and Dan Keller

Although most scholars believe this song was written by next door neighbors Keller and Higley in 1873, it was never copyrighted and has been subject of several lawsuits. Harmonica-wise, while you'd think it's an easy one, it's not—mainly because it's set so high. You may find it easier to play on a harp set in a lower key, perhaps an "A" or a "G." There is also a low-end version of this song notated in Chapter Six.

## Prepare Yourself Before You Start To Play

Think of a song as being a little like an athletic event for which you need to prepare yourself both mentally and physically. Take a couple of breaths to help relax and clear your mind. Lick your lips so they're nice and lubricated. Cup your harp lovingly and get a sense of the way you're going to pace yourself. Wait until you feel ready. Finally, when that little voice says *now*, calmly and confidently start to play.

*Circled means draw*
*Uncircled means blow*
*• means tongue*

# Yankee Doodle – Traditional

C                 G    C          G

7  • ⑧ 8 7   8 ⑧   7 • ⑧ 8 7 ⑦

Yankee Doodle went to town, riding on a pony,

C          F          G          C

7    • ⑧ 8 ⑨ 8 ⑧ 7   ⑦   6 ⑥ ⑦ 7 •

Stuck a feather in his cap and called it maca–roni.

F                    C

⑥ ⑦ ⑥ 6 ⑥   ⑦ 7   6 ⑥ 6 ⑤ 5 6

Yankee Doodle keep it up, Yankee Doodle dandy,

F                 C     G    C

⑥   ⑦ ⑥ 6 ⑥ ⑦ 8   ⑥ 6   7 ⑦ ⑧ 7 •

Mind the music and the step, and with the girls be handy.

Although the origin of "Yankee Doodle" has been claimed by France, Spain, The Netherlands, Germany and Hungary, the melody seems to have come from England where it was a children's game called "Lucy Locket." And what is "macaroni?" It's an insulting term to describe the feather coming out of Oliver Cromwell's hat. "Yankee" was a contemptuous nickname the British had for New Englanders, and "doodle" a similar term meaning "dope." Despite all this, the colonists took up this song as their call to arms and sang it at their many victories during the Revolutionary War. Unfortunately, it has to be played on the high end of the harmonica (see "Problem Holes") but is still great fun.

## Lack of Confidence is No Reason Not to Learn

The greatest artists are almost always the most insecure—at least at first. Even if you have low confidence, keep going, have fun, and refuse to deny yourself the pleasure of music.

MARINE BAND

Circled means draw
Uncircled means blow
• means tongue

# Dixie – Dan Emmet

C

4 • • ④ 5 ⑤ 6 • • 5

Wish I was  in the land of cotton;

F

⑥ • • 6 ⑥ 6 ⑥⑦

old times there are not forgotten.

C                    G    C

7 ⑧ 8 7  6 7 6  5 6 ④ 5 4

Look away, look away, look away, Dixie Land!

                              F

7 4 • • • ④ 5 ⑤ 6 • • 5 ⑥ • • 6 ⑥ 6 ⑥⑦

In Dixie Land where I was born in, Early on one frosty morning,

C                    G    C

7 ⑧ 8 7  6 7 6  5 6 ④ 5  4

Look away, look away, look away, Dixie Land!

            F        D      G

7 • • 8 ⑧ 7 ⑥ 7 ⑥⑧ ⑥⑧

Then I wish I was in Dixie, hooray! hooray!

C            F            C            G

6 7 8 ⑧ 7 ⑥ ⑦ 7 ⑥ 6 5 7 5 • ④

In Dixieland I'll take my stand to live and die in Dixie.

   C  G  C

5 4 5 ④ ⑤ 5 4  8  7 ⑧ 7

Away, away, away down south in Dixie,

   C  G  C              G C

5 4 5 ④ ⑤ 5 4  8  7 ⑧ 7

Away, away, away down south in Dixie.

Dan Emmet was a minstrel musician—a talented violinist who played his fiddle deliberately out of tune and wrote many of the great songs of this era. When Abe Lincoln first heard this song, he shouted from his box, "Let's have it again!" Within a few years, however, this ditty had been appropriated as the march song of the Confederacy.

## Learn the Difficult Art of Bending Notes ✳

The next tune includes a note that is, technically, not on the ten-hole diatonic harp. You can get this note, however, by bending the 3 draw. * means to play the note in the "bent" position. Because the note for the word "side" is not on the harmonica, you need to hit this note by bending the 3 draw. This intermediate harp technique is described in detail in the next chapter. If you're a raw beginner, not ready for bending yet, fake it by substituting 4 draw for the 3 draw bent.

4/4 time

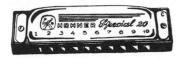

*Circled means draw*
*Uncircled means blow*
• *means tongue*
* *means bend*

# Londonderry Air (Danny Boy) — Fred E. Weatherly

        C        Cm⁷                F        Fm

③4 ④ 5 ④ 5 ⑥ 6 5 ④4③* 4
O Danny Boy, the pipes, the pipes are call–ing,

                C      Am               Dm  G

4 5 ⑤6 ⑥ 6 5 4 5 ④
From glen to glen and down the mountainside.

               C       Cm⁷             F       Fm

③ 4 ④ 5 ④ 5⑥ 6 5 ④4③*4
The summer's gone and all the flow'rs are dy – ing,

              C       G         F C

③ 4 ④ 5 ⑤ 5 ④4④ 4
'Tis you, 'tis you must go and I must bide.

                        F           C

6 ⑥ ⑦ 7 ⑦ • ⑥ 6 ⑥ 6 5 4
But come you back when summer's in the mea–dow,

                  F               G  G⁷

6 ⑥ ⑦ 7 ⑦ • ⑥ 6 5 ④
Or when the valley's hushed and white with snow.

              C    F          C     Em Am

6 • • 8 ⑧ • 7 ⑥7 6 5 4
'Tis I'll be here in sunshine or in sha – dow.

             C           F    G    C

③4 ④ 5 ⑥6 5 ④ 4③* ③ 4
O Danny Boy, O Danny Boy, I love you so.

And if you come when all the flowers are dying,
And I am dead as dead I may well be,
You'll come and find the place where I am lying,
And kneel and say an ave there for me.
And I shall hear, so soft your tread above me,
And then my grave will warmer, sweeter be.
For you will bend and tell me that you love me,
And I shall sleep in peace until you come to me.

Weatherly, an Englishman, wrote these lyrics to "Londonderry Air" an old Irish tune. O.K., it's not an American song, but once you learn to bend the 3 draw, it's a gorgeous song for the harmonica.

## Really Listen To Yourself Play (As You Play)

Spend a few minutes listening critically. Is your tone cramped? Is it hissy? Make adjustments in your face, lips, the tilt of your harp, how far the harp is in your mouth, and the direction of your airstream until your tone is improved.

*3/4 time*

Circled means draw
Uncircled means blow
• means tongue
* means bend

# Auld Lang Syne – Robert Burns

      C               G

3     4  ③ 4  5  ④ 4 ④

Should auld acquaintance be forgot,

     C             F

5  4 • 5     6 ⑥

And never brought to mind,

        C           G

⑥   6  5 • 4  ④ 4 ④

Should auld acquaintance be forgot,

5 ④ 4  ③* • 3  4

    F            C

In    days of auld lang syne.

          G         C      F

⑥ 6  5 4 ④ 4 ④ ⑥ 6 5 6 ⑥

For auld lang syne my dear, for auld lang syne,

  C           G        F        C

⑥  6  5 • 4 ④ 4  ④ 5 ④ 4  ③* 3 4

We'll take a cup of kindness yet, for    auld lang  syne.

> We two have run about the braes & put the gowans fine.
> We've wandered many a weary foot for auld lang syne.
> For auld lang syne, my dear, for auld lang syne,
> We've wandered many a weary foot for auld lang syne.
>
> We two have sported in the burn frae morning sun 'til dine,
> But seas between us braid have roared for auld lang syne.
> And here's a hand my trusty friend & give a hand of thine,
> We'll take a cup of kindness yet, for auld lang syne.

In the late 1700's Robert Burns, the great Scottish poet, copied this song of friendship and time from an old man's singing and added two verses himself. Incidentally, in Scots Gaelic "auld lang syne" means "long time since."

## Spend Another Moment Improving Your Tone

The deeper you park that harpoon between your relaxed, puckered lips the better your tone will be. The larger your single note hole, and you're still able to get a single note, the sweeter and richer your tone. Just like you can't be too thin or rich, your tone can't be too unspeakably beautiful. Take time to make that harp throb!

*3/4 time*

*Circled means draw*
*Uncircled means blow*
*• means tongue*
*∗ means bend*

# Star Spangled Banner — Francis Scott Key

```
      C          Am   E⁷    Am    D    G   G⁷
6 5   4   5   6   7   8  ⑧   7     5   6*  6
Oh  say can you see, by the dawn's ear-ly  light,
```

```
           C         G      G⁷         C
6   •   8  ⑧  7   ⑦       ⑥ ⑦  7  •   6   5   4
What so proudly we hailed, by  the twilight's last gleaming?
```

```
 C                        Am      E⁷       Am  D⁷  G  G⁷
6     5     4    5    6    7    8   ⑧  7 5  6*   6
Whose broad stripes and bright stars through the peril-ous fight,
```

```
        C          G      G⁷       C
6   •   8  ⑧   7  ⑦      ⑥  ⑦ 7 •  6   5   4
O'er the ramparts we watched were so gallantly streaming.
```

```
                                      G
8  •   •  ⑨  9   •   ⑨  8    ⑧ 8 ⑨ •
And the rocket's red glare, the bombs bursting in air,
```

```
     C              G  G⁷    C   D      G  G⁷
⑨   8   ⑧   7   ⑦ ⑥ ⑦  7   5   6*  6
Gave proof through the night that our flag was still there.
```

```
     C              F         Dm                 G
6 7  •   •⑦ ⑥   •   •  ⑧ 8 ⑨ 8 ⑧ 7 •⑦
Oh say does that  Star-Spangled Banner   yet    wave
```

```
        C  Am   C  Am     C   G    C
6   •   7 ⑧ 8  ⑨  9   7  ⑧  8  ⑨⑧  7
O'er the land   of the free and the home of the brave?
```

The bent 6 blow indicated by 6∗ is an unusual technique used to compensate for the missing half-step between 5 draw and 6 blow. To bend 6 blow, push the air forward and down. To fake it, play 6 draw instead of the bent 6 blow. You can also play our national anthem on the low end of the harp, bending 2 draw and 3 draw (see next chapter). Neither is easy, but make great practice. When you can combine the high end with the low end, people will pay money to hear your version. Play ball!

## Turn Your Tongue Into a Rhythm Machine

The simple act of tonguing, when done crisply in the front of your mouth, can make your rhythm jump. Try it first on your airstream without the harmonica. Then add the harp and play this song like a drum!

⁴/₄ *time*

*Circled means draw*
*Uncircled means blow*
*• means tongue*
*\* means bend*

# Down by the Riverside – Traditional

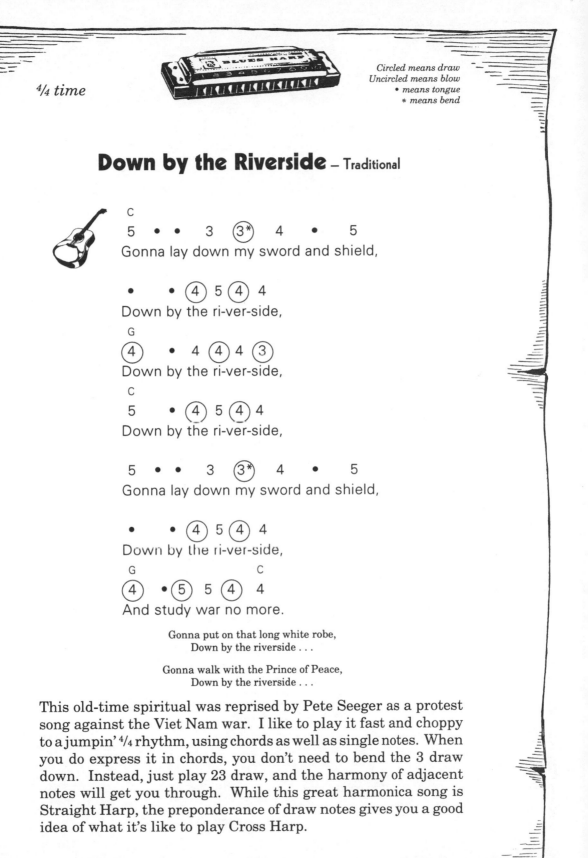

C
5 • • 3 ③\* 4 • 5
Gonna lay down my sword and shield,

• • ④ 5 ④ 4
Down by the ri-ver-side,

G
④ • 4 ④ 4 ③
Down by the ri-ver-side,

C
5 • ④ 5 ④ 4
Down by the ri-ver-side,

5 • • 3 ③\* 4 • 5
Gonna lay down my sword and shield,

• • ④ 5 ④ 4
Down by the ri-ver-side,

G            C
④ • ⑤ 5 ④ 4
And study war no more.

Gonna put on that long white robe,
Down by the riverside . . .

Gonna walk with the Prince of Peace,
Down by the riverside . . .

This old-time spiritual was reprised by Pete Seeger as a protest song against the Viet Nam war. I like to play it fast and choppy to a jumpin' ⁴/₄ rhythm, using chords as well as single notes. When you do express it in chords, you don't need to bend the 3 draw down. Instead, just play 23 draw, and the harmony of adjacent notes will get you through. While this great harmonica song is Straight Harp, the preponderance of draw notes gives you a good idea of what it's like to play Cross Harp.

## Play Harmonica in Curves

Make the sliding and swiveling movements of the harp, the reversal of breath, the intensity of your notes, and the dance of your hands fluid and smooth. Make the notes blend into each other. Play it in curves, baby.

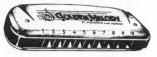

*3/4 time*

Circled means draw
Uncircled means blow
• means tongue
* means bend

# Swing Low, Sweet Chariot – S. Sheppard

G     C   G     C     G                Em         D

(3)   3   (3)   3 • 2 (1)   3 • • • (3)(4) 5 (4)

Swing low, sweet char–i–ot,     coming for to car-ry me home.

         G               C     G             Em      C   G

5 (4)(3)   (4)   3 • 2 (1)   3 • • • (3) 3 2   3

Swing low, sweet char–i–ot,     coming for to car-ry me home.

G                            C        G

(3)(4)   3 • • • •   • • • (1)

I looked over Jordan and what did I see?

                  Em     D

3   • • • (3)(4) 5 (4)

Coming for to car-ry me home.

G                   C       G             Em     C G

(4) 5 (4)(3) 3 • • • • (1)   3 • • • (3)(2) 2   3

A band of angels coming after me.   Coming for to car-ry me home.

If you get there before I do, coming for to carry me home.
Tell all my friends I'm coming too, coming for to carry me home.

In 1847, on hearing that she'd been sold and would be separated from her baby, Tennessee slave Sarah Sheppard was stumbling towards the Cumberland River, vowing suicide. A prophetic old woman stopped her: "Wait! Let the sweet chariot of the Lord swing low. There's a great work for this baby to do on earth." Sarah went home and let herself be sold into Mississippi, while her baby girl stayed behind. This is the song she wrote and sung for her daughter. Thirty years passed. In 1878, her adult daughter, Ella, now one of our first successful, classically-trained black musicians, began a search for her mother and, once reunited, took the older woman to live with her. It's also said that this song is about the "underground railroad." Whatever the origin, it's one of our very best. Incidentally, it is presented in the Cross Harp Style. (See next chapter.)

## Don't Stop Playing. Period.

The only people who don't learn to play better are those who quit.

So don't quit!

Circled means draw
Uncircled means blow
• means tongue

# When the Saints Go Marchin' In

C
4   5   ⑤   6     4   5   ⑤  6
Oh, when the Saints  go marchin' in,

                                     G   G⁷
4   5   ⑤   6   5   4   5   ④
Oh, when the Saints go marching in,

              C                       F
5   •   ④  4   •   5  6   •   •   ⑤
Oh Lord, I want to be in that number,

              C           G      C
4   5   ⑤   6   5   4   ④  4
Oh, when the Saints go marchin' in.

And when the sun refuse to shine,
And the moon refuse to rise,
Oh Lord, I want to be in that number,
When the Saints go marchin' in.

And when the harmonica players start to play,
And it sounds so gosh darn good,
Oh Lord, I want to be in that number,
When the harmonica players start to play.

Originally, this song was deeply and religiously spiritual. Created by slaves who performed it on drums, jawbones, and bamboo tubes in the middle of the 19th century, it was picked up by the Holy Rollers, a religious sect known more for dancing and singing than bible-reading. Later, it became a speciality at New Orleans funerals where, after the ceremony, the burial musicians and the crowds would dance, strut and sing, and jam on their trumpets, tubas, and drums all the way back to town. Later, it became a Louis Armstrong jazz trademark and an international favorite, which, of course, it still is today.

## Your 3-Part Learning Program

Divide your learning system into three parts!

1. **The time you spend exploring something new.**
   This might be a new song, or a song you've avoided in the past because it was difficult. It could be learning to bend the 3 draw so you can play "Danny Boy," or just wandering around the harp looking for melodies of your own. When working with new material and techniques, keep your expectations low, and move on to number two.

2. **The time you spend improving something you've started.**
   You've learned the notes to "Turkey in the Straw," but it still sounds stilted and slow. Isolate the first line and play it again and again until it's up to lip-burning speed. Then move on to the second line, the third, fourth, and so on. In every practice session keep improving your material. Like a snowball, it builds.

3. **The time you spend *listening* to recordings or live concerts of great harp players.**
   Open yourself up to the music around you, but don't be intimidated. Instead, try to get the sounds you hear into your memory and imagination. Try to feel the beauty of the experts in your own less-developed musical voice. They may have superior technique and talent, but no one owns the franchise on feeling and soul.

# Chapter Six

# Blues, Bending and Beyond

### An inquiry into the more advanced skills of modern-day harmonica playing

*"I'd been playing harmonica since I was
a little baby, but I'd never heard anyone play it
the way that stranger played it.
Man, he made that thing talk. We was sitting in a
boxcar and it all made sense, him playing like a
train and us riding a train. Him huffin' and puffin'
as the countryside rolled by with the stars and
the moon flashing through the trees. We went by
a river and he played a river. Went through a field
and he played a field. I had my harpoon
wrapped up in a bandanna and I kept asking him
how he done that music, but he wouldn't
stop playing long enough to show me.
It wasn't 'til years later I figured it out for myself."*

# Secrets of Bending Notes

"Bending" is the skill of taking one note, say, 4 draw, or 3 draw, or 2 draw, and directing the airstream down into your throat to actually *lower* the note. On holes 1 through 4, you can bend only the draw notes. On holes 7, 8, 9 and 10, you can bend the blow notes. The most important bends, however, are 2, 3 and 4 draw, with 4 draw being the one people usually start on.

Bending is definitely one of the keys to mastering the mystique of the harmonica. It's difficult to explain and, for most of us, difficult to master. When you demonstrate it for people who know nothing about harp, it generally astounds them. And when they hear it in the midst of someone playing, it drives them wild.

The first thing I want to tell you about learning to bend is to be patient. This could take you a few minutes, or a few years. Once again, the key is in the single note—usually figuring out a way to place the harp still deeper within your puckered lips to get a pure, clear unimpeded tone.

It's tempting to tell you to work on this, and to let the bending emerge naturally. While this is good advice, it's also true you paid good money for this book and probably want me to try to explain. O.K. As the best danged harp teacher in the modern world, I'll do better than explain, I'll get you bending! First, play a 4 draw single note. Make it your best single note, deep within your puckered lips. Now, the bending action is like a exaggerated inhaled whistle that starts high, and swoops low.

Or, starts low, and swoops up.

Or, starts off in the bent position and stays there.

As you play your 4 draw, try to imagine it bending in the ways I just described. Hear it in your mind, then do it!

## "The Hiss"

"The Hiss" is a teaching technique that's very successful for getting beginners to bend. The first step is to put down your harp, and *draw* air through your puckered lips so you produce a loud snake-like hiss. Because it's coming through your perfect pucker, the hiss should have kind of a "wh" sound to it, like an inhaled *whisssssssss!*

Now don't do this just one time. I want you to get good at it. Make that hiss last five seconds. Pucker those lips and notice that as you change the shape of the pucker, the sound of the hiss changes. What I want you to do is fine-tune the pucker so your hiss is loud, real loud, and so you can make the sound last several seconds.

## The 'weeeuuuu' Sound

You need to have a sense of power in your hiss. Control and focus the airstream so it's cooling the inside of your lips and the roof of your mouth. Even though it will sound more like an rapid airleak from a balding bicycle tire than the vowel sound, think the vowel sound *weeeeeeee* as you do it. This is how you play a note in its straight-up, unbent position.

Now, to bend a note down, the airstream starts off hitting your lips, and then hits the roof of your mouth. Then you **flip, jerk, force** the airstream down into the back of your throat. This flipping back into your throat actually occurs as you open the throat up to receive the air. This is similar to the vowel sound *ewe* or *uuu!*

So, still working **without the harp**, make your loud, long, drawn hiss airily enunciate the vowel sounds *weeeuuu* As you do this, move the focus of air from the insides of your lips to the open hollow of your throat.

**Do not do this by collapsing your pucker.** Instead, open your throat and feel the power of the air pressure down there. This is not rocket science. It is not talent. It's a knack. Truly no more difficult than whistling. Work on it until you've got it. *weeeuuu! weeeuuu! weeeuuu!*

Once you feel as though you've got the hang the hissed *weeeuuu!* take a moment to analyze how you're doing it. I want you to feel and label this for yourself, but I can give you a clue. As you go from the *weee* to the *uuuu*, the rear of your tongue drops, your throat hollows out, and the hiss changes sound. Close your eyes and climb into your own mouth and throat. Is that how it happens for you? Try to figure it out for yourself as you powerfully hiss the *weeeuuu* again and again.

## From Hissing to Bending

You're probably way ahead of me on this one. Put the harp back in your mouth, get a deep puckered single note on your 4 draw. Now, make that airstream go from *weee* to *uuu*. Remember to do this powerfully. Focus the air at the front of the mouth and change that focus to your hollowed-out throat. Even though the bend seems to happen in your throat, it's *initiated* with a slight twisting of lips. Come on, do it . . .

Four draw unbent . . . bent . . . unbent. Do this again and again. If you get a lily-livered *la la la* feeling, you're wiggling your tongue. Return to the hissed *weeuuu* without the harp. Power! Think power! Then try it again with the harp. If you get a bend that turns into a high squeak, you're bending too hard. Too much power! Either back off, you beast, or you'll break the reed!

Try it again. Put that harp deep into your puckered lips and get a beautific single note on 4 draw. Now bend. *Weeeuuu!* Yes! That's how you do it!

Once you've got it on the 4 draw (easy for me to say), try it on the 3 draw and the 2 draw. The bends here are even more difficult which is why there's so much more instruction ahead. Nonetheless, if you're bending the 4 draw at this point, you should be proud. This is not easy stuff.

If you're not bending yet, try not to get too frustrated. It took me years to learn. And always, always, always, return to the deep puckered single note—because that's the key.

# Doc's Guide to Best Bending Notes*

**1 draw:** Great special effect note with the capacity to drop one step. On a C harp, that's D to D flat. Good for imitating contented cows mooing.

**2 draw:** One of the hardest notes to play (has a tendency to sound like a fog horn) yet has the incredible bending capacity to give you three notes. On your C harp these are G, F sharp and F. Along with it's neighbor, 3 draw, 2 draw is the star of advanced harp playing. (More on this later.)

**3 draw:** A big thick note that needs to be honked back into your throat to bend. On the C harp, there are three possible notes in the wonderful 3 draw—B, A and A flat. Bending to hit that A note is the key to playing many low end melodies. Hitting the A flat is the key to blues.

**4 draw:** The D note can actually drop to D flat, a hair-step above the 4 blow. This is a big note to bend and unbend in blues and country music and is the first note most people learn to bend.

**6 blow:** Rarely used; this easy blow-bend makes "Star-Spangled" come alive.

**6 draw:** One of the easier notes to bend, and along with 4 draw, a good place to start.

**7 blow:** On C harp, this is a C note, where most of your Straight Harp songs begin and end. A fun way to play it is to start beneath the note and swoop gracefully up to the unbent position.

**8 blow:** On your C harp, 8 blow can bend E to E flat. Wonderful for emotional melody playing.

**9 blow:** One of the last notes most people learn to bend. On a C harp, G bends to F sharp. Sounds great once you've got it. While learning it's pretty shrill. Doc's suggestion: Learn to bend the high notes on a low key harp such as the G or A.

**10 blow:** So high on a C harp most folks can barely play it, let alone bend it, though there are those who do.

* This guide does not include the overblow bends recently created by Howard Levy.

# For Those of Us with Problems on the Low Draw Notes

(and more help on bending)

*"What the x?/#%!!!! is wrong with my 2 draw?"*

You might think I'm hitting this pretty hard, but I want to get it across—2 and 3 draw are two **of the most important notes on your harmonica.** When playing Straight Harp melodies, the ability to play them with good tone in both bent and unbent positions lets you to play songs and scales that were previously possible only above 4 blow.

When playing Cross Harp and the blues (explained later), being able to bend and unbend these two notes gives you instant soul.

But here's the rub—2 and 3 draw are also probably **the most difficult notes on the harp**. Often, these two rascals come out sounding like foghorns, or worse, refuse to play at all. Sometimes there's a high-pitched shriek, as though the reed were screaming in defiance. For certain players, frequently there's a feeling of resistance, as though the air can't move through the hole. Or, if air can come through, the resulting note is flat, distorted and generally unpleasant to play and hear.

The temptation now is to draw harder. To force that note out whether it likes it or not. The result of this macho tug of war is usually increased resistance, and sometimes, a permanently damaged reed. Uh, oh! Time to buy a new harp. Now's when many people who would otherwise become good harmonica players quit. Or, they never learn to play 2 draw and 3 draw correctly, and doom themselves to a lifetime of not-so-great harp playing.

Why not-so-great? Because if 2 draw or 3 draw won't produce clear, unbent single notes, you're probably playing *all* your drawn single notes in a slightly bent, flattened position. The result is flat-out lousy tone all over the harmonica. On the other hand, if you learn to play 2 and 3 draw correctly—unbent, clear and unrestricted—your tone, mastery and playing pleasure will be improved on all the holes of your harp—plus, now you'll be in a position to learn the correct way to bend notes.

## 2 and 3 Draw—The "Sensitive" Notes

More than any other holes on the harp, the 2 and 3 draw have the quality of *bendability* in them. Once you know how, they bend deeper and lower and more dramatically than any of the others. What many frustrated beginners are doing is bending these sensitive holes unintentionally. That's why they sound like fog horns. The trick now is to learn to unbend them!

When working with the following suggestions, try playing 2 and 3 draw single notes for periods of at least six seconds (or beats) at a time. This gives you a chance to make adjustments in your breath, mouth-shape and overall approach during each attempt. And remember, **your goal is to get a clear, unbent, unblocked single note on 2 or 3 draw.**

1. If you are at all frustrated (and who wouldn't be?), calm down. Smile. The harmonica is a lady who won't respond to anger or force. Ask her nicely.

2. Pucker to make your single note aperture (the shape your lips form to get the single note) as large as possible (higher then wide). Place your harmonica inside your lips, not on the edges.

3. Gently draw on hole 2 or 3, and see how your tone is. If it seems blocked or resistant, **don't stop drawing.** Simply try cutting the volume of air in half, and . . .

4. . . . consciously direct the airstream **up** so it feels as though you are drawing air **through your nose.** At the same time, **lighten** your clamp on the harmonica. Don't suck the air through the harmonica. *Guide* it. Don't force the air through the harmonica. *Coax* it.

5. Relax your lips and jaw and throat more. One way is to tighten them as much as you can, and then allow them to go flaccid.

6. Make sure your lips aren't reaching for the harmonica. Instead, **pull the harmonica up into your face, and also lift the harmonica up towards your nose.** In other words, lift everything.

7. Before you get filled up on the draw, gently blow into the same hole, and long before you run out of breath on the blow, gently draw. Keep your breath going, in and out, in and out, as you work with the above suggestions. If you stay **controlled and focused,** it won't be long before those notes come ringing through, clear and undistorted.

## Suggestions For Bending

Only when you're satisfied with the clarity and ease of your unbent single notes on 2 and 3 draw is it time to start learning to bend. I know we've already talked about the *weeeeuuuu* approach and that's a good one to try. Here's another way to think about it. Since you were already bending the 2 draw and 3 draw unintentionally and getting a foghorn sound, try returning a bit to that blocked-up feeling. Try to do with your air what you were doing when 2 draw and 3 draw felt resistant, and use the resistance as you draw the air to shape your sound and to make it lower.

For instance, on 2 draw, feel the focus of the note and the direction of the airstream at the top of your head, **unbent.** Now pull the note and the airstream down into your throat, **bending it.** Then release the tension and the note by directing the air back up to the top of your head, **unbent.**

Another, very subjective way to think about this is: Try going from **guiding** the air to the top of your head, to **sucking** it down into your throat, back to **guiding** it. Unbent, bent, then unbent. When trying to bend the 2 and 3 draws you are liable to come up with the most ungodly, disgusting sounds. That's it! That's what you're trying to do! I frequently coach my students with exhortations like "Manhandle that note!," "That's right, suck it down. Force it down!"

## Once You Have A Bend* . . .

. . . start working with it. Get to know it and make it yours. For instance, play 3 draw and bend it down as far as it will go. Pause to silence.

Then play 3 draw again, but start at the bottom of the bend and bring it up.

Do this several times. Now, play only the bent 3 draw. This is the note you need to play "Danny Boy" and "Auld Lang Syne" and many other songs.

Try the same exercise on 2 draw. Learn to play 2 draw in the bent position and the unbent position. Yes, there will be some distortion. Use your hands to minimize it.

Here's a list of challenges:

- Learn to bend 2 and 3 draw so you can play the scale from 1 blow to 4 blow.

- Learn to bend 2 draw and 3 draw just right so you can play the melodies on the low end of the harp.

- Learn to bend 2 and 3 draw just right so you can play the blues.

- Learn to bend the high notes just right so they don't sound screechy and weird.

- Integrate all this into your music and become a great player, rich and famous.

- Tell them you learned it from me and send me money.

- Lots of it.

---

\* Many times people learn to bend more easily with their hands cupped.

# Honking Those
# Two and Three Draw Bends

The trick to playing melodies on the low end of your harp is in mastering the 2 draw and 3 draw bends. This is demonstrated most clearly in the notation for "Auld Lang Syne," "Star Spangled Banner," and "Danny Boy." In these songs, you need to be able to bend the 3 draw or the 2 draw (or both) down and play these notes in their "bent positions."

You accomplish this by practice and patience. Your first goal is to bend the note. Your second goal is to learn to play it in the bent only position. The third goal is to play the bent note in an undistorted manner with perfect pitch so that it sounds as though it's just another note on your harmonica. The reward is being able to play songs that usually have to be played on the high end of your harp on the middle and low ends. Bending is also an essential tool in the blues harp sound.

As mentioned earlier, there is not a *do re mi* diatonic scale on the low end of your harp—unless you can bend the 2 draw and the 3 draw down to hit the "missing" notes. If you master this, you're on your way to some pretty advanced harp playing. Warning: this is strong medicine!

### Straight Harp Scale — Low End    *\* means bend*

| 1 | (1) | 2 | (2*) | (2) | (3*) | (3) | 4 |
|---|-----|---|------|-----|------|-----|---|
| do | re | mi | fa | sol | la | ti | do |

| 4 | (3) | (3*) | (2) | (2*) | 2 | (1) | 1 |
|---|-----|------|-----|------|---|-----|---|
| do | ti | la | sol | fa | mi | re | do |

On the following page are some versions of tunes you already know. Working with them will help you perfect these low draws.

## Bill Bailey – Low End

2 • ①  2  ① 2 3  2  • ①  2
Won't you come home Bill Bailey?  Won't you come home?

3  •  2 3  ③* ①
She cried the whole night long.

②*• 2 ②* 2 ②*② ②* • 2 ②*
I'll do the dishes, honey.  I'll pay the rent.

②  •  •③* 3  2
I know I done you wrong.

2  •  • ①  2① 2  3  2 •  ①  1
Remember that rainy evening, I drove you out,

4  •  •  •  •④ 4  ③*
With nothing but a fine tooth comb?

4 •  • ③* 4  5  •  ④ 5 ③*
I know I'm to blame.  Well ain't that a shame?

4  • ③* 4  ③* 5  •  4
Bill Bailey, won't you please come home?

## Turkey in the Straw – Low End

5  ④ 4 • ④ 4  2 ②*②③* 3 2  3
Well, I had an old hen, and she had a wooden leg,

4  ④ 5  •  •  4④ 5 • ④ 4 ④
Just the best old hen that  ev–er laid an egg.

5  ④ 4 •④ 4  2  ②*② ③* 3 2 3
Well, she laid more eggs than any hen on    the farm,

4 ④ 5 6 •⑥ 6 5 4  ④ 5 4 ④ • 4
But another little drink wouldn't do her an–y  harm.

5  6 • • •  5  6  •
Turkey in the hay, hey, hey hey.

⑤⑥ • • •  ⑤  ⑥  •
Turkey in the straw, straw, straw, straw.

⑥  ⑦ 7 •  • 6 • • 5  • ④
Pick 'em up, shake 'em up any way at all,

4④ 5 6 • •  5 4 ④ 5 4 ④③  4
And  hit up a tune called  a  Turkey in the Straw.

143

*means bend*

# Battle Hymn of the Republic – Low End

3 • • • ②\* 2 3 4 ④ 5 • • ④ 4
Mine eyes have seen the glory of the coming of the Lord,

4 ③③\* • • ③ 4 ③
He is trampling out the vintage

4 ③\* 3 ③\* 3 2 3
where the grapes of wrath are stored.

3 • • • ②\* 2 3 4 ④ 5 •• ④ 4
He's loosed the fateful lightening of his terrible swift sword,

4 ④ • 4 ③ 4
His truth is marching on.

3 ②\* 2 3 4 ④ 5 4 ③\*③ 4③ 4 ③\* 3 2
Glory, glory hal–le–lu–jah, Glory, glory hal–le–lu–jah,

3 ②\* 2 3 4 ④ 5 4 • ④ • 4 ③ 4
Glory, glory hal–le–lu–jah, His truth is marching on.

# Home on the Range – Low End

3 • 4 ④ 5 ④ 4 ③\*⑤ • •
Oh give me a home where the buffa–lo roam,

5 ⑤ 6 4 • •③ 4 ④
And the deer and the antelope play,

3 • 4 ④ 5 ④ 4③\* ⑤ • •
Where seldom is heard  a  discouraging word,

⑤ • 5 ④ 4 ③ 4 ④ 4
And the sky is not cloudy all day.

6 ⑤ 5 ④ 5
Home! Home on the range.

3 • 4 • • •③ 4 ④
Where the deer and the antelope play,

3 • 4 ④ 5 ④ 4③\* ⑤ • •
Where seldom is heard  a  discouraging word,

⑤ • 5 ④ 4 ③ 4 ④ 4
And the sky is not cloudy all day.

*means bend*

## Star Spangled Banner — Low End

3 2 1 2 3 4 5 (4) 4 2 (2*) (2)
Oh say can you see, by the dawn's ear-ly light,

3 • 5 (4) 4 (3) (3*) (3) 4 • 3 2 1
What so proudly we hailed, by the twilight's last gleaming?

3 2 1 2 3 4 5 (4) 4 2 (2*) (2)
Whose broad stripes and bright stars through the peril-ous fight,

3 • 5 (4) 4 (3) (3*) (3) 4 • 3 2 1
O'er the ramparts we watched were so gallantly streaming.

5 • • (5) 6 • (5) 5 (4) 5 (5) •
And the rocket's red glare, the bombs bursting in air,

(5) 5 (4) 4 (3) (3*) (3) 4 2 (2*) (2)
Gave proof through the night that our flag was still there.

3 4 • • (3) (3*) • • (4) 5 (5) 5 (4) 4 • (3)
Oh say does that Star-Spangled Banner yet wave

3 • 4 (4) 5 (5) 6 4 (4) 5 (5) (4) 4
O'er the land of the free and the home of the brave?

## Yankee Doodle — Low End

4 • (4) 5 4 5 (4) 4 • (4) 5 4 (3)
Yankee Doodle went to town, riding on a pony,

4 • (4) 5 (5) 5 (4) 4 (3) 3 (3*) (3) 4 •
Stuck a feather in his cap and called it maca–roni.

(3*) (3) (3*) 3 (3*) (3) 4 3 (3*) 3 (2*) 2 3
Yankee Doodle keep it up, Yankee Doodle dandy,

(3*) (3) (3*) 3 (3*) (3) 4 (3*) 3 4 (3) (4) 4 •
Mind the music and the step, and with the girls be handy.

145

# Playing and Bending the High Notes

Before you've discovered the knack of bending notes, it seems impossible. Hour upon frustrated hour passes as you try again and again to get more than a silly waver in your tone. Just as you're about to give up and donate your harmonica to your favorite charity, you do something new and natural with that drawn airstream. To your astonishment , the note you've been torturing suddenly bends down and back up. Jumping Jehovah! You've got it! You can bend! Then you wonder why you ever thought bending was so hard.

This is what I went through as I learned to bend—especially the high notes. I had been good on the low notes for years, but holes 7, 8, 9 and 10 were a mystery to me—so much so that I didn't even mention them in my first book. Playing harp on holes 1 through 6 was hard enough!

Then one day I heard some kid playing the high end in Balboa Park in San Diego, and he was good. Damned good. I had to admit that these notes *could* be played and bent by a mere mortal, and set about learning to do it. What totally surprised me was that blow notes could be bent on holes 7, 8, 9 and 10. The first step was to get a good single note on these tough high notes. Once that tone came ringing through, I could bend the note by pushing the airstream forward and down.

So now it's you're turn . Take your time. Bring patience to the party because you're going to need her. I recommend you start with hole 8, getting a good single note, and then trying to bend it by pushing the air forward and down. It will also help you to use a lower key harp such as A or G . While you're at it, here's the . . .

## High End Scale

7   (8)   8   (9)   9   (10)   10*   10

do   re   mi   fa   sol   la   ti   do

This is challenging. In addition to the mechanical difficulties of getting a sound from these holes ( let alone bending them), you need get used to the idea that on hole 7 and above, blows are higher than draws which is the reverse of the way it is from holes 1 to 6.

Another important point for the aural safety of your friends and neighbors, children and pets: **avoid making these notes too shrill**. Control your volume and mellow out the screeches by cupping your hands behind the higher notes. Good luck!

## Auld Lang Syne – High End

6      7  ⑦ 7  8    ⑧ 7 ⑧
Should auld acquaintance be forgot,

8   7  •  8      9  ⑩
And never brought to mind,

⑩    9    8  •   7    ⑧ 7⑧
Should auld acquaintance be forgot,

8⑧ 7  ⑥  •  6   7
In     days of auld lang syne.

⑩ 9   8 7 ⑧  7  ⑧  ⑩ 9   8 9 ⑩
For auld lang syne my dear, for auld lang syne,

⑩   9   8 •  7 ⑧  7  ⑧  8⑧ 7  ⑥6 7
We'll take a cup of kindness yet, for   auld lang  syne.

# When the Saints Go Marchin' In – High End

7  8    ⑨ 9     7  8  ⑨  9
Oh, when the Saints go marchin' in,

7  8    ⑨ 9    8 7  8   ⑧
Oh, when the Saints go marching in.

8  •  ⑧7  •  8 9 •  •   ⑨
Oh Lord I want to be in that number,

⑨ 8   ⑨ 9    8 7  ⑧  7
Oh, when the Saints go marchin' in.

# Doc's Magical Musical Theory Made Simple

*definitely not a piano*

Now the good Doc's going to give you something kind of chunky to chew on—his version of easy music theory. True, it's a bit oversimplified, and also true, you don't really need to be an expert on this subject to play harp. Nonetheless, here's a general overview of how music works and where the harmonica fits in. I've left out some of the mettlesome details such as sharps and flats etc.

## Here we go . . .

1. Music is made up of vibrations that strike the eardrum and are heard as sounds, or tones. This vibration can be made by someone singing, striking the back of a frying pan with a spoon, a guitar string buzzing, cowpoke belching, a free-standing reed humming—even a horse neighing. What's important is that once it hits the eardrum, the vibration becomes a **tone.** The lower tones are those that vibrate slowly, and the higher ones vibrate quickly.

2. Somewhere along the line of Ancient Musical History, some European or Middle Eastern musician-type decided to identify each tone and give it a name that could be communicated to other musician-types. So, he took the lowest tone he could find and called it an "A" and the next highest one, a "B" and so on. You could say this was the "civilizing" of music because now it could be written down. From this point on, the tones were known as **notes,** which is probably short for "notation." That's why we identify the tones with the words, "A note," "B note," "C note" and so on.

3. Now let's move into **scales,** which is what the melodic part of music is organized around. Think of a scale as a ladder of notes with the rungs set in particular places. The most common and basic of these scales is the one that goes **do re mi fa sol la ti**

**do.** This ladder has eight rungs, also referred to as whole steps, and is known as the **diatonic** scale. Through-out history and in different cultures, other scales are used, some with fewer steps and others with more. A more complex scale is known as the **chromatic** (basically a diatonic scale with six half-steps between the whole steps) and is used in the more sophisticated musical forms such as jazz and classical. A more simple scale is the **pentatonic** ( five whole steps) which frequently forms the basis of blues.

4. So that's what a scale is, and the scale I want you to think about at this point is the diatonic. From here, let's talk about the **key** the music is in. You can end a scale, or a song, on any note and probably say correctly that that's the key you're playing in. For instance, if you end on an A note, it's usually an A scale, and the key is A. If you start and end on a C note, it's usually a C scale, and the key you are in is C.

   You can play or sing a song in any key. "Shenandoah" can be played or sung in the key of A, the key of C or the key of F sharp. (Whoops! I wasn't going to bring in sharps and flats, but since I have, let's just say that sharps and flats are halfway between the "whole" notes. For instance, F sharp is halfway between the notes of F and G.)

5. Here, at point five, Doc's Theory gets a little bit more complex, so stay with me. If you play the first, third, and fifth notes of a scale (any key) at the same time, the resulting sound is a **major chord**—a pleasing combination of harmonizing notes that join together to create one united whole. If you do this on an A scale, you get an A chord. On a C scale, you'll play a C chord. You can hear this by playing 123 blow or 456 blow. This combination of notes creating **a harmony and a chord** is one of the great miracles of music, and to a musician one of the great miracles of life. Like seeing a rainbow, having a baby or falling in love— **harmonies and chords** are proof positive that the world is indeed a beautiful place.

6. Whew! We've made it all the way into chords. Let's talk about **chord progressions,** which are used to create the structure of a song. The most popular arrangement in Western music is the **I-IV-V progression.**

Generally speaking it's the guitar or piano that plays these chords and the harmonica-player who accompanies. Here's how she works . . .

> **The I Chord:** Playing in the key of C, this is a C chord.
>
> **The IV Chord** is up 4 steps—**1-C**, 2-D, 3-E, **4-F**—and is an F chord.
>
> **The V Chord** is up 5 steps—**1-C,** 2-D, 3-E, 4-F, **5-G**— and is a G chord.

Playing in the key of C, you generally start with the C chord for four or eight beats, go to the F chord for a few beats, then to the G chord and finally finish the song on a C chord. This is an over-simplification, but does give you an idea of what's typical. For a more realistic view, check out the guitar chords in the songs of **Harmonica Americana.**

7. So that's chord progressions. Your mission, as a harp player, is to play melodies, or groups of harmonizing notes that express or accompany the chord progression (which is usually played by a guitar or a piano.) When you play the **core melody,** this happens automatically. When you **improvise,** you "discover" which notes harmonize with the core melody. Luckily for those of us who love to change things around, the harmonica's arrangement of notes is ideal for improvisation or vamping. More on this in the next section.

# Straight Harp Accompaniment and Improvisation

O.K. So what's so special about the unique tuning of the harmonica?

If you were to drag your hand across a piano keyboard or the strings of a guitar, you would produce a confused, unmusical sound, almost like an orchestra tuning up. That's because these instruments possess all the notes of all the different keys—and with your random drag of your hand, you're basically playing in twelve different keys at the same time.

Ugh!

On the other hand, when you randomly blow and draw on your harmonica, you get mostly pleasing, harmonious sounds that fit with each other. That's because the ten-hole harmonica, for the most part, only gives you the notes that belong to the key you're playing in.

This mono-keyed approach to the instrument presents you with the disadvantage of not having all the musical notes you might need to play a particular piece. (Say, "Flight of the Bumblebee" or "How High the Moon.") This is a frequent frustration for harp players, a limitation we learn to live with.

On the other hand, your simple harp has the advantage of allowing you to play pleasing, harmonious sounds all over your instrument. This means you can accompany a guitar or keyboard quite freely simply by accenting the root notes and the harmonizing notes. And hallelujah, playing Straight Harp, **every blow note is either a root note or a harmonizing note.**

What's a root note? It's the first note of the key you're playing in. Playing Straight Harp, your **root notes are always 4 blow, 1 blow, 7 blow and 10 blow**. These are usually the notes that songs end on.

**Harmonizing notes** (other notes which will always work) are the other blow notes: **5 blow, 6 blow, 8 blow, 9 blow, 2 blow and 3 blow.**

In other words, when playing Straight Harp, you can confidently play background to your guitar player by playing patterns that accent the blow, and in almost all cases, you will **never** make a mistake. By "accent," I mean to play these notes with more emphasis, and to end your patterns on them. Examples of patterns or riffs that will always work when accompanying a guitar or piano are:

**Meadow Lark Melody Run:**          5  ④  4
(you can play this fast over and over)

**High Meadow Lark Melody Run:**     8  ⑧  7
(can be played fast over and over)

**Straight Harp Ascender:**          4  ④  5  6  7  ⑧  8

**Straight Harp Descender:**         8  ⑧  7  ⑥  6  5  4

One more point: If your guitarist is playing a song in the key of A, you need an A harmonica in order to play Straight Harp. If he's playing in the key of C, you use a C harmonica. And so on.

# Song Improvisations

Let's imagine a great soul singer like Ray Charles or Aretha Franklin recording a song like "Auld Lang Syne" or "America, the Beautiful," or even "Mary Had a Little Lamb." Do you think Ray or Aretha would sing these songs exactly the way children sing them in grade school? Or would they change the melodies so their voices could take off, wailing, warbling, stretching out to hit high notes, swooping low to hit low notes, and basically turning the song inside out to create something new, exciting and joyful? My guess is number two. They'd take off and *improvise*.

And that's what I want to talk about now. To improvise means "to improve upon" and is one of the great joys of playing any instrument, especially the harmonica. You start off with a basic song, and then, through an act of courage, foolishness, imagination, and a desire to seize the musical moment you "take off" and make the song yours.

To help you understand how this works, I'm presenting you with the notation for "improvisational" versions of "Auld Lang Syne" and "America the Beautiful." They probably will make more sense when you hear them on the tapes that accompany this book. But this much is for sure—these versions leave the exact melody far behind as they unite the high and middle sections of the harp to give a new twist on old songs. They sound best when used to accompany guitar and piano and are certainly subject to modification.

Being able to improvise on a melody and play the entire harp, holes 1 through 10, is one of the goals of learning the high, middle and low ends of the harp. So, if you're ready for a new challenge, put this in your harp and play it . . .

# Auld Lang Syne — Improvisation

3    4 ③ 4  5  ④ 4 ④
Should auld acquaintance be forgot,

5  4  •  5    6 ⑥
And never brought to mind,

9   ⑨ 8 ⑧ 7  ⑥ • 6  5 ④ 4
<u>Should auld acquaintance be forgot</u>,

④ 5 ④ 4 ③* 3   4
<u>In   days  of</u> auld lang syne.

⑥ 6  5 4 ④ 4 ④ ⑥ 6  5 6 ⑥
For auld lang  syne my dear, for auld lang  syne,

9   ⑨ 8 ⑧ 7 ⑥ • 6   5 ④ 4 ④ 5 ④ 4 ③* 3  4
<u>We'll take a cup of kindness yet,</u>    <u>for auld</u>    lang    syne.


# America the Beautiful — Improvisation

6  •  5 • 6  •  ⑥  ④
Oh beautiful, for <u>spacious</u> skies,

5 ⑤ 6 ⑥ ⑦ 6    5 6 ⑥ 7 ⑥ 6
for amber waves of grain,    (<u>pause, pause</u>)

6  •  5  •  6  • ⑤ ④ ⑧ 7  ⑧ 8 ⑥ ⑧
For purple mountain majesties  above thy fruited plain.

6 8 ⑧ • 7 • ⑦ •  7  ⑧ ⑦ ⑥ 6   5 4 ④
Ame–ri–ca, Ame–ri–ca, God <u>shed his</u>    <u>grace on</u>   <u>thee</u>.

④ 5 6 ⑥ 7 ⑥ 6
(<u>pause, pause</u>)

9  ⑨ 8 ⑧ 7 ⑥ • 6 ⑥   7 ⑥ 6
<u>And crown    thy good   with brotherhood</u>,

⑥   7    6 ⑧ 9
<u>From sea to shining  sea</u>.

## "America, the Beautiful" Improvised

 My approach to improvisation is to play a song correctly the first time through. That way my listeners know what song I'm playing, and they also know that I know how to play it! Now I feel more free to take off on the melody, trying to follow the basic structure and feeling but also playing different notes than what you'd expect.

I use three basic principals to improvise on a melody. They're "Note Substitution," "Embellishment," and "Riff Substitution." Using the notation for "America, the Beautiful," let me explain:

## Note Substitution

On the syllable "<u>ious</u>" in "spacious," I've notated a **6 draw** instead of the **5 draw** the melody calls for. This simple substitution of one note another presents a pleasant and jazzy surprise.

## Embellishment

After the word "grain" there's a pause that lasts two beats. I've utilized this pause to embellish the melody with a quick pattern of notes that fits with the flow of the song. This adds another element of surprise to the song, and suggests that I know what I'm doing as a harp player (which is *really* a surprise!)

## Riff Substitution

At the word "shed" I boldly depart from the melody, taking a made-up pattern of notes (a riff) from 8 blow down to 4 blow and then up to 9 blow. The main requirement for this musical departure is that it has similar timing as the core melody and that many of the main notes are shared. Although some musicians may create this effect by figuring it out ahead of time, I just take off as I play and see where it leads me. This is how I came up with this "improvisation" and it's definitely the way improvising works best for me.

# Cross Harp—Wailing the Blues

We've taken Straight Harp **Harmonica Americana** pretty far—all the way into improvising and jazzing up some of the greatest tunes of all time. Now the good Doc wants to back up a little bit and briefly introduce you to something that's easier than Straight Harp improvisation, and harder than Straight Harp melodies—and that's Cross Harp or "Second Position."

More than anything, Cross Harp is a feeling. It's the bluesy, wailing, soulful low-down, gutsy, gritty, get-down, talk-to-me-baby, midnight rambler, jazz-sweetie style of harp-playing. It's the talking harp. It's the lonely train whistle. It's country harp. It's folk harp. It's rock harp. It's blues harp. It's rhythm harp. It's everything today's harp is famous for, and once you can play Cross Harp, man, you can stop traffic!

But let's say that even after the incredibly well-written description above you still aren't sure what Cross Harp sounds like. Your next step might be to do some listening. My suggestion is that you use the resources in the back of this book to pick up some blues and country-western albums or tapes. I want you to hear the big, fat amplified sound of Little Walter, or Charlie McCoy's Cross Harp country melody style, and the droning, chord-based folk music of the great Sonny Terry.

I want you to hear Tom Ball, Rick Estrin, Mickey Raphael and Charlie Musslewhite. I want you to hear the guy in your town band who nobody's ever heard of, but is just as good as these famous guys. (Ahem! You might also want to pick up some of Gindick's instructional books and tapes. He's not so bad himself.) Whoever you end up listening to, getting the sounds of Cross Harp into your mind and body will go a long ways towards helping you get the sounds of Cross Harp into your harmonica.

## How's It Work?

First, let's take a look at Straight Harp:

When you **blow** on holes 1, 2, 3 and 4 of your C harp, you play a C chord. Go ahead and give this a try.

This is the musical basis for Straight Harp and songs of **Harmonica Americana.** You play your C harp in the key of C, and the music you get is based on the diatonic scale of our European-based musical past. The result is melody-making, a great approach to the harp.

But what about our African tradition? What about the story-telling *griots* from that great and mysterious continent thousands of miles south of Europe? What about the blues and those evocative falling-tones described in Chapter One? That's where Cross Harp comes in, and here's how it works. **When you *draw* on holes 1, 2 3 and 4 of your C harp, you play a G chord. When you play Cross Harp, you base your music on this Big Draw Chord. You end up playing your C harp in the key of G, and accenting the draw notes.**

While most Straight Harp songs begin and end on 4 blow or 7 blow (C notes on your C harp), **Cross Harp songs usually begin and end on 2 draw or 3 blow or 6 blow** (G notes on your C harp), and the overall accent is on the draw notes, in particular 4 draw, 3 draw, 2 draw and 1 draw.

Here are four songs, easy to play in the Straight Harp style, now notated in the more difficult Cross Harp style.* To play these songs all the way through, you need to be able to bend the 3 draw and 2 draw down a entire note. If you can't convincingly bend these notes yet, you're not alone. This is advanced stuff, probably part of your Five Year Harmonica Plan. Work as best you can with the notation and you'll get a meaningful introduction to the feelings and techniques of this powerful way of playing harmonica.

---

\* An easier Cross Harp song is "Swing Low, Sweet Chariot," notated on page 129.

# When The Saints Go Marchin In — Cross Harp

3 ③ 4 ④ 3 ③ 4 ④
Oh when the saints, go marchin' in,

3 ③ 4 ④ ③ ② ③ ③*
Oh when the saints go marching in.

③ • ③* 3 • ③ ④ • • 4
Oh Lord, I want to be  in that number,

③ 4 ④ ③ ② ③* 3
When the Saints go marching in.

# Amazing Grace — Cross Harp

① ② ③ • ③* 3 • ①
A-maz-ing grace how sweet the sound,

① ② ③ • ③* ④
That saved a wretch like me.

③ ④ 5 • ③ ③* 3 • ①
I    once was lost, but now I'm found,

① ② ③ • ③* 3
Was blind but now I  see.

## Red River Valley – Cross Harp

(1)　(2)　(3)　•　•　•　(3*)(3)(3*) 3
From this valley they say you are going,

(1)　(2)　(3)　(2)　(3)　(4)　4　(3)　(3*)
We will miss your bright eyes and sweet smile.

(4)　4　(3)　•　(3*) 3 (3*)(3)　(4)　4
For they say you are taking the sunshine,

(1)　•　•　(2*)　(2)　(3*)(3)　(3*) 3
That has brightened our pathways awhile.


## Shenandoah – Cross Harp

(1)　(2)　•　•　(3*)(3)　4　5　(4)
Oh Shenandoah, I long to see you.

6 (4)　5　(4)　5　(4)(3)(4)
A – way you rolling ri–ver.

(3)(4)　6　•　•　(3)(4)(3)(3*)　3
Oh　Shenandoah, I long to see you.

(1)(2)　(1)　(2)　5　(4)
A-way, we're bound a-way,

3　(3*)(3)　(2)(3*) 3
Cross the wide Missouri.

# Doc's All-Purpose Blues and Country Cross Harp Riffs

Even if you can't yet play "Shenandoah," "Red River Valley," "When the Saints Come Marchin' In," or "Amazing Grace" in the Cross Harp style, I hope *trying* to play them helps you hear and feel the potential of Cross Harp. You see, until you get really good, Cross Harp is generally not used to play songs exactly the way they were written. **Instead, it's used for jamming and playing riffs, bluesy patterns of notes you use when improvising on songs.**

A typical blues jam might be:

> Singer: "My baby left me this morning!"
>
> Harp riff: "Wah wah ta wah!"
>
> Singer: "I don't know what to do!"
>
> Harp riff: "Waaaah wah wahwah ta ta wah!!!!!!"

The *wa wa* part of the scenario above can be handled in a variety of ways. Since Cross Harp accents the low draw notes, the harp player may want to make sympathetic sounds on 1 draw, 2 draw, 3 draw, or 4 draw. He or she may want to bend these notes, or tongue them or use cupped and uncupped hands to help mold these sounds to the music.

Or, the harp player may use one or more of "Doc Gindick's All-Purpose Country and Blues Cross Harp Riffs," including:

| | |
|---|---|
| The Up Riff: | 3 ③ 4 ④ |
| The Down Riff: | ④ 4 ③ 3 |
| The Four Draw Surprise: | ④ 4 ③④ |
| Good Morning Riff: | ① 2 ② 2② |
| Bent Three Draw and Blow Boogie: | ③* 3 |
| Six Blow Down: | 6 ⑤ ④ 4 ③ 3 |

These are just a few of the Cross Harp riffs you can use for both country and blues. To learn more (and you should!), pucker up to any of my books, tapes or videos on Cross Harp. These materials will let you hear how the riffs sound and give you blues and country guitar music for your practicing pleasure.

## The Secret Cross Harp Formula

Once again, when you play Cross Harp, you're not playing your C harp in the key of C. You're playing it in the key of G, accenting the draw notes instead of the blow. That's the trick, the Secret of Cross Harp.

Now for the Cross Harp Formula—the way to know what key you're playing in when you play Cross Harp. One way is take a look at your harp. What key is it in? A? C? G? Let's say you have a C harp, that you want to play Cross Harp, and you need to tell your guitar player what key to play in. The formula is to **count back four steps from the key the harp is in.** (It's O.K. to use your fingers.) For instance:

| Harp | | | Guitar |
|------|------|------|--------|
| C | B | A | G |
| 4 | 3 | 2 | 1 |

and tell your guitarist to play in the key of G.

Let's say you have an F harp. Count back four steps . . .

| Harp | | | Guitar |
|------|------|------|--------|
| F | E | D | C |
| 4 | 3 | 2 | 1 |

and tell the guitarist to play in the key of C.

The chart on the next page does this simple calculation for you. On the left is the key that the music (the guitarist) is in. This is also the key you use to play Straight Harp. To play Cross Harp, use the harmonica listed in the right hand column. Put the accent on those draw notes and wail.

## Cross Harp Conversion Chart

Key of Music

| Straight Harp | Cross Harp |
|---|---|
| **(1st Position)** | **(2nd Position)** |
| A | D harp |
| B flat | E flat harp |
| B | E harp |
| C | F harp |
| D flat | F sharp harp |
| D | G harp |
| E flat | A flat harp |
| E | A harp |
| F | B flat harp |
| F sharp | B harp |
| G | C harp |

## Train Imitations and Hound Chasin' Fox

It's three years down the line and you've mastered the songs of Straight Harp Americana. You've mastered Cross Harp blues and country. As a result, you've ascended to staggering heights in the world of music and now you're playing at halftime at the Superbowl in the largest stadium in the world.

The place is pitch-black except for the revolving spotlights and the flickering flames of the thousands, no, tens of thousands, of lighters and matches signaling the crowd's support for you and your music. With your little C harp in hand you approach the microphone.

Overhead, the blimp seems to come closer, and as you bring your harp to your mouth, that worldwide audience in radio and TV Land takes a collective breath. What will you play? Shenandoah? Turkey in the Straw? A Cross Harp blues?

No! It's your famous train imitation. A riveting, rhythmic *chuggalugga, chuggalugga* that has the audience up on its feet dancing, clapping, shouting, singing! My word, what hath your harp wrought? The place has gone nuts!

Now the football players are coming out on the field. They can't stand it! Their touchdown victory dances are nothing compared to the music *you're* making! Off come the helmets. Off come the pads! They're dancing! Dancing with each other! The football commissioner is waving his arms! He's dancing with the union organizer! A little old lady is streaking across the field! Naked! And still your harp wails *Woo! Woooo! chuggalugga chuggalugga Woo! Woooo!*

＊　＊　＊　＊　＊　＊　＊

Make no mistake: Train music and fox and hound imitations are some of the most exciting forms of harp playing. And if you learn to create this excitement on your harmonica, you and you alone will be responsible for the consequences. Trust the ol' Doc here, when people hear this fast rhythmic stuff on the harp, they go wild.

## Using Chords to Create a Groove

So how do you do it? First, this music is as individual as the person making it so use my instructions as a jumping-off point. Secondly, this music is played Cross Harp, usually using chords 1234 draw and 1234 blow to create a musical groove. Stomping your foot to the 4/4 beat, give each blow and draw a count of one beat. Try this over and over. That's it! Make it musical!

(1234)　1234　(1234)　1234　(1234)　1234　(1234)　1234　**(repeat)**

The most common problems people have with this are:

1. **Lousy tone:** The solution is to hold the harmonica very lightly in your mouth with your lips loose. Also: cut the volume of air in half. No need to play loudly. You may want to reread "First Sounds."

2. **Getting filled up with air:** The solution is to open your mouth wide on the blow and empty your lungs by blowing hard over the top of the harmonica. As a matter of fact, it's best if ninety per cent of the air goes over the top of the harp. You should get a loud hiss when you do this, and this is okay because the sharp staccato hiss adds to the realism of a train and is also quite rhythmic.

Try mastering the draw and blow/hiss groove using the suggestions above. Take it nice and easy, not too fast, and give it a rhythmic, musical swing as opposed to a mechanical, machine-like thrashing.

## Add Tonguing

Is it musical yet? Can you do it nice and easy for two or three minutes at a click? Well, keep working on it and remember that the key for musicality might be to play it really soft. Also remember to keep your mouth loose with the lips barely touching the harp. That said, the next step is to use tonguing to articulate the draw chord. Although there are hundreds of ways to do this, let's start with the following pattern. As you work on it, you may discover a way that you like better. Until then . . .

. . . as you draw 1234, tongue the syllables *ah taaa ta*. Then blow (air over top of harp). Then draw, tonguing *ah taaa ta* again. Repeat one hundred times. O.K., fifty times!

(1234)       **1234**      (1234)      **1234**  **(over and over)**

**ah taaa ta**          **ah taaa  ta**

A word about the tonguing—the first syllable *ah* is simply the sound of 1234 draw untongued. As you make this sound, you tongue the *taaaa*, and tongue once again, making the shorter *ta* . . . and blow-hiss, making most of the air go over the harp. Without a moment's hesitation, you draw and do it all again.

Your goal is to find an easy pace that lets you play smoothly. Part of this is achieving a balanced breathing pattern so you can play for a long period of time. That hissing air going over the top of the harp is a big part of this balance.

Let yourself learn by going slow, like a train pulling out of the station and chugging across the countryside at an even, leisurely clip. Then when you get good at it, let the speed build, and build, and build, and build . . .

## Whistles Moaning, Hound Dogs Howling

By now, you've got a pretty good rhythmic groove, using either Doc's tonguing pattern or one of your own. It's at this point that you decide whether this little piece is a fox and hound chase in which the hound is chasing the fox and you can hear that old dog barking, or whether to stay in the train motif with the train whistle, the steam hissing out from the wheels and the conductor calling "All Aboard!"

If this is a train imitation, you need a train whistle. The best one I've found is the one you get when you jump up to holes 45 draw and play this as a chord that lasts, say, four beats, using your hands to get the best possible tone, then lightly bending and unbending the notes for that wailing, lonesome sound.

You can do this, say, five times in a row before jumping back into your 1234 draw and blow groove. If you want, move the groove up a hole so you're doing it on holes 2345 draw and blow. Then up another hole and another after that. Finally work your way down, going faster and faster and faster. Make that train whistle wail. Then slowly lose speed, coming into the station and, finally, to a complete stop.

Now that's the train imitation. The fox and hound chase is very similar except that you deliberately try to put the sound of dogs barking into your music. I do this by alternating the sound of my voice going *haa* with the sound of a draw chord or a draw single note. (It took me years of practice to do this poorly.) I'm also able to get a bark-like sound by honking on my 2 and 3 draws, bent and distorted in just such a way that, if I'm having a good day, a feral feeling comes ringing through. As in all harp playing, if you think dog, you'll probably get a sound like a dog. Think train, you'll probably get a train. The harp is great in that way.

Again, the most important part is getting an intense rhythmic groove going and building your own unique piece out of that. It may sound like a ten car pufferbelly out of a Currier & Ives print hauling down the line. It may sound like a garbage truck banging its way down a suburban street. It may sound like a hound chasin' a fox through the Bayou. It may sound like a purple-haired old lady's French poodle yapping at a mailman. It may sound like the hooves of galloping horses racing across the desert on a starlit night. Or, it may sound like the old mare on her last legs baying *he haw* at the moon!

Whatever your music is sounding like these days—pull out your harp and do it. Do it right now.

# The Grand Reward

Well, folks, we've made it to the end of the book, you and I.

I hope you're having some real fun with your harp, on your own level, in your own way. Let's go back to square one with the question, "I've got this harp here. What should I do with it?"

Doc's suggestion? **Play it.**

Even if you're just starting out—**play it!**

Even if you don't like how it sounds yet—**play it!**

Even if you have no musical background whatsoever—**play it!**

There's nothing sweeter than being in a beautiful location (or even an ugly one!) taking your harp from its case, lovingly cupping it in your hands, puckering up for a sweet single note, and playing the opening to a great song with a clear, strong, rich tone that seems to resonate through space, bouncing off the clouds, returning to your ears like a kiss from the Creator.

So stay with your harmonica. Keep practicing and playing. If someday, sitting beside some waterfall or mountain stream, or in some echoing stairwell of some sterile highrise, or even sitting in the car next to you in some lonesome freeway traffic jam, you see a curly haired fellow playing some sweet **Harmonica Americana,** pull out your harp—and join him.

I can't wait to hear you play.

Your harp pal,
Jon "Doc" Gindick

Give a friend a memorable day
Play a song for him on the harmonica.
Even modestly played,
the sound of the harmonica spreads joy
and makes happy memories.
Better yet, start your own class
and teach others to play.
You don't have to be a great player—
just a patient teacher with the ability
to express and share enthusiasm.

# Doc's Guide to Harp-Playing Resources

*"I worked with Doc's book and thought I had the
harp pretty well figured out. But I wanted more.
So I sent away for the stuff in the next chapter,
plugged into a bigger harmonica world,
and what a world it is!*

# Additional Resources for Harp Players

**American Harmonica Newsletter** (Al Eichler, editor) 2362 W. Territorial Road, Battle Creek, MI 48906.

**Harmonica Information Publication** (Winslow Yerxa, editor) 203 14th Ave., San Francisco, CA 94118.

**Kevin's Harmonica Resource Guide** (Kevin McGowan, editor) 210 Farnsworth Ave., Bordentown, NJ 08505. (800) 274-2776.

**Mississippi Saxophone** (Tim Moody, editor) 3672 Game Farm Road, Springfield, OR 97477. (503) 726-5992.

**Easy Reeder** (Toni Radler, editor) c/o Hohner, Inc., Post Office Box 15035, Richmond, VA 23227.

**Harmonica Happenings** Society for the Preservation of the Harmonica (SPAH), Post Office Box 865, Troy, MI 48099. (SPAH can tell you of a harmonica club in your vicinity.)

**Harp-L** (Internet harmonica subscriber service) Send e-mail to <majordomo@garply.com> with message "subscribe Harp-L."

**Joe Filisko Custom Harmonicas** 1313 Colorado Avenue, Joliet, IL 60435.

**National Harmonica League** (Colin Mort) Rivendell, High Street, Shiiel Heath, Southhampton SO3 2JN, England.

## Mail order music companies for blues and country recordings are:

**Roots and Rhythm,** 6921 Stockton Ave., El Cerrittos, CA 94530. (510) 525-1494

**Elderly Instruments,** 1100 N. Washington, Lansing, MI 48099. (517) 372-7890

**Alligator Records,** Post Office Box 60234, Chicago, IL 60660. (800) 344-5609

# Doc's Great Cassette Lessons . . .

Especially performed by Doc for **Harmonica Americana,** these two equally wonderful 60-minute teaching lessons will get you playing and learning your harmonica anywhere there's a cassette player . . . in your car, your home, even while walking! They let you hear what you're playing, keep you motivated and make harp learning fun.

## Harmonica Americana Volume I
## "Basics"

Learn to play the great songs notated in **Harmonica Americana,** as Doc gives you slow-motion, step-by-step instruction on single notes, hands, tonguing, bending, playing the songs and more. You'll be referring to this taped hour for general harmonica improvement including inspiration, motivation, specific techniques, Doc's exercises, and a darn good harmonica time. Recorded in stereo for your C harp. A steal at $9.50.

## Harmonica Americana Volume II
## "Jam Along Songbook"

Here's Doc on his sweet-sounding ol' Martin guitar, playing his harp, and strummin' that big chord of C. He goes through the great songs—"Danny Boy" to "Turkey in the Straw" to "Old Folks at Home" to "Shenandoah" and all the rest—bringing them to life and letting you hear and play along with these American masterpieces. The entire tape is recorded in stereo for your C harp and will get you, your friends and family singing and playing along. Larceny at $9.50.

## Price Break!

Get both tapes for $18. Book included, $24.95. "C" Harmonica, $10 extra. Book alone, $11.95. Please add $3 shipping on all orders. Call or write for quantity discounts.

# Play Cross Harp!

**The Natural Blues and Country Western Harmonica** Book and cassette lesson series by Jon Gindick

With over 200,000 books sold since it was first published in 1977, **The Natural Blues and Country Western Harmonica** is a friendly, funny 130 page book by best-selling harmonica instruction author Jon Gindick. This method is easy, fun and, as thousands of accomplished harp players now testify, it is the easiest, most common sense way to learn basic blues harp ever devised.

With help of great illustrations, funny cartoons and clear explanations, you'll receive simple, effective instruction on single notes, tonguing, bending, using hands, playing the world's easiest blues and country riffs, jamming with guitar, and much more. Included is a record index to tell you what key of harp you need to jam with over 100 popular records. This "bible of blues harp instruction" is just **$7.95.**

**Cassette Lesson I** gives you slow-motion examples and step-by-step instruction on every technique and riff described in the book. For C harp. . . . . . . . . . . . . . . . . . . . . . . . .$9.50 (With book $13.95)

**Lesson II** This 60-minute cassette includes games and exercises that help you loosen up your mouth and discover the music that's already in you. For C harp. . . . . . . . . . . . . . . . . . . . . . . . . . . .$9.50

**Lesson III** is a 60-minute instruction tape that explains and takes you through the riffs of the I-IV-V progression.
For C harp. . . . . . . . . . . . . . . . . . . . . . . . . . . . . . . . .$9.50

**Ol' Willie's Melody Cassette** explains and plays the 26 songs notated in The Natural Blues & Country Western Harmonica book. For C harp. . . . . . . . . . . . . . . . . . . . . . . . . . . . . . . . . .$9.50

## Blues Harp, The Movie

**Country and Blues Harmonica for the Absolute Beginner**
An instructional video by B.B. King and Jon Gindick

Jon Gindick and blues guitar legend B.B. King made this superb video—to let you **hear** and **see** detailed instruction on how to play the blues harp.

Face to face, harp to harp with Jon , you'll go over the basics—holding the harp, lip shapes for single notes, how to bend notes, tonguing notes, using your hands. Then you'll jam with B.B.—the man many call the most influential blues guitarist of our time.

**60 minutes of blues harp instruction for $24.95. VHS or Beta.**

## Rock n' Blues Harmonica

book and cassette series by Jon Gindick

This acclaimed 224-page book is an extraordinary journey into the heart and soul of harpin.' Included is harp theory, playing chord cycles, beginning and advanced technique, playing with bands, playing straight, cross, slant styles—and much more. A record index tells you the harp keys to jam with 100 albums. . . . . . . . . . . . . . . . . . . . . . . . . . . . . . . . .$14.95

**Rock n' Blues Beginner's Lesson** This 60-minute tape teaches the basic techniques and riffs. For C harp $9.50
With book . . . . . . . . . . . . . . . . . . . . . . . . . . . . . . . . . . . . . .$19.95

**Rock n' Blues Accompaniment Lesson** is a *tour de force* of instruction and playing for beginners and intermediates. 45 minutes. For C, D, A, G harps. . . . . . . . . . . . . . . . . . . . . . . . . . . .$9.50

**Three Chords of the Blues** is a jam-along lesson that teaches and demonstrates every chord cycle in the book. 50 minutes. For C and G harps. . . . . . . . . . . . . . . . . . . . . . . . . . . . . . . . . . . . . . . . .$9.50

## More Taped Lessons from Jon Gindick

**Harp and Guitar Jam Vol. 1**
Jam with Jon to seven different guitar chord progressions. Includes country, jazz, rock, folk and blues styles.
G and C harps. 60 minutes . . . . . . . . . . . . . . . . . . . . . . . .$9.50

**Harp and Guitar Jam Vo.l 2**
Features blues, boogie, rock jams, and many tips on bending, and tongue-blocking and riff making.
For A harp. 60 minutes . . . . . . . . . . . . . . . . . . . . . . . . . .$9.50

**The Four Positions of Blues, Rock and Jazz Harmonica.**
Learn the secrets of 4th position (C harp in key of E), Straight Harp Blues (C harp in the key of C), Cross Harp melodies (C harp in key of G), 3rd position riffs and melodies (C harp in key of D minor). Includes easy guitar music for all four styles.
60 minutes . . . . . . . . . . . . . . . . . . . . . . . . . . . . . .$9.50

**The Robert Johnson Lesson**
Teaches you seven Robert Johnson blues classics. Includes "Rollin' and Tumblin,'" "Sweet Home Chicago," "Love in Vain" "Come in My Kitchen," " Dust My Broom," and "Walking Blues."
For C harp . . . . . . . . . . . . . . . . . . . . . . . . . . . . . . $9.50

**Gospel Plow**
This two-volume set teaches the Cross Harp way to play gospel standards "What a Friend We Have in Jesus," "Kum Ba Yah," "When the Saint's Come Marching In" and many others.
. . . . . . . . . . . . . . . . . . . . . . . . . . . . .$14.95 for two tapes.

## DISCOUNTS

Cassettes are $9.50 for 1, $18 for 2, $26 for 3, $34 for 4, $41 for 5, $47 for 6, $54 for 7, $60 for 8, $65 for 9, $5 for each additional.

Send your check, money order or credit card info to:

**Jon Gindick, 530 Ranch Road, Visalia, CA 93291**

**Add $3 shipping to all orders.** California: add current sales tax.
Overseas: add enough shipping for airmail.